Synagogue Song in America

I raise my hands to God on High,
With offer mixed, as day draws nigh;
Accept my praise while Evensong,
Whose time is fixed, Thou do prolong.

Mas'at Kapai, 13th century,
Mordechai ben Shabatai.

Synagogue Song in America

Joseph A. Levine

White Cliffs
Media Company

Crown Point,
Indiana

White Cliffs Media Company
P.O. Box 561
Crown Point, IN 46307

Library of Congress Catalog Number: 88–17178

∞ Printed on acid-free paper in the United States of America.

Library of Congress Cataloging in Publication Data

Levine, Joseph A., 1933–

(Performance in world music series ; no. 4)
Bibliography: p.
Includes index.
1. Synagogue music—United States—History
and criticism. 2. Chants (Jewish)—History and criticism.
I. Title. II. Series.
ML3195.L48 1988   783.2'096   88–17178
ISBN 0-941677-12-5
ISBN 0-941677-14-1 (pbk.)

C O N T E N T S

Recapturing the Art of Synagogue Song
Sacred chant knits Jewry together. Its influence
and components are described.

PART I: PSALMODIC TECHNIQUE

Jerusalem of Old
Second-temple practice emphasized words over music,
and likely recitation over singing. This pattern spread
to synagogues in Judea and the diaspora, paralleling
early Christian singing.

Climbing the Liturgical Ladder
The liturgy becomes more complex as it moves from
weekday to Sabbath to Festival to High Holy Day; so
does its music, retaining its Psalmodic underpinnings.

PART II: BIBLICAL TECHNIQUE

Tone Density; Neumes; *Misinai* Tunes
Biblical technique is slower-paced and louder than
Psalmodic technique. Its figurations (neume motifs) vary
in every diaspora community; they spawn one group
reverently called *Misinai* ('from Mount Sinai') Tunes.

List of Musical Examples

CHAPTER ONE

CHAPTER TWO

CHAPTER THREE

CHAPTER FOUR

CHAPTER FIVE

CHAPTER SIX

CHAPTER SEVEN

CHAPTER EIGHT

Acknowledgments

Synagogue Song in America links theory to practice, and should interest both lay readers and professionals. It is the first book to isolate four basic components that form Jewish liturgical chant, and to rationally reassemble them. It breaks new ground, upon which I hope others will build. Although intended as an accessible reference work showing the Americanization process at work in Synagogue song, the book will also serve as a practical guide for musicians and scholars of all faiths.

Because this overview of Synagogue song is meant for a general—as well as scholarly—audience, a simple system renders the original Hebrew into readable phonetics: Werner Weinberg's *General Purpose Romanization of Hebrew for Speakers of English*; adopted by the American National Standards Institute, 1975. Weinberg's system is especially welcome for presenting textual underlay in musical examples. Since most accents have been eliminated, the reader is free to concentrate on marks pertaining to the music. For the Hebrew itself I follow Sephardic pronunciation, due to its prevalence in American synagogues. Popular usage also explains my choice of the Lithuanian tradition as reference for Biblical chant (Appendix B).

Webster's *Third New International Dictionary* provided spellings for well-known names, customs, events, functionaries, and generic terms. The *Revised Standard Version* of the Bible was my source for Scriptural quotations. In translating prayer-texts, I have borrowed from collections too numerous to mention here.

This book owes much to my former students at the Jewish Theological Seminary of America, whose encouragement (and healthy skepticism) kept me going during the early phases of research. The findings of authorities such as Abraham Idelsohn, Eric Werner, and Hanoch Avenary have been invaluable, as have the scholarly suggestions of Johanna Spector, Max Wohlberg, Raymond Scheindlin, Hugo Weisgall, and Israel Katz. I am also indebted to Marsha Edelman, Judit Frigyesi, Lawrence Loeb, and Larry Smith, who read the manuscript and shared their ideas with me. Although I have incorporated many emendations from all those mentioned above, the ideas and methods in this book are my own, and are not necessarily endorsed by my colleagues or publisher.

My editor, Michael Scofield, deserves a literary medal of honor for standing his ground until I produced a single-field theory that made sense. My wife, Doris, has earned her share in the World to Come by seeing me through the difficult transition from performer to critic.

The cooperation of Baltimore Hebrew University and its President, Dr. Leivy Smolar, allowed this work to see the light of day.

Most of all I wish to acknowledge a friend and colleague who worked with me in organizing the initially unwieldy data, first as individual lectures, then as a series of articles. The sudden death, on March 13, 1982, of this brilliant and compassionate man left an unfillable void on the Jewish musicological scene. In the spirit of his lifelong pursuit—study for its own sake—I dedicate this effort to the memory of Dr. Albert Weisser.

Joseph A. Levine
Philadelphia, PA, 1989

PREFACE

Recapturing the Art of Synagogue Song

The men of Great Faith have passed on . . .
Mighty were they to stand
in prayer before thee,
suppliant of pardon and forgiveness,
scattering the clouds of disaster,
and saving our people from peril.

Anshei Emunah, 13th century,
Meyer the Younger

Recapturing the Art of Synagogue Song

F̲ewer and fewer American cantors know how to perform traditional Synagogue song or *chazanut*. Yet Hebrew prayer as expressed through sacred chant—spanning 30 centuries—encompasses the soul of Jewry's strengh. In this Preface we will discuss the influence of Synagogue song in the past, consider its current status in the Jewish community, and propose a method for its revitalization.

Synagogue Song in the Past

Historically, cantorial singing has played an acknowledged role in Jewish life, as illustrated by the following literary examples. For several centuries following the Jewish expulsion from Spain and Portugal (1492–1498), cantorial duties comprised a true ministry, including the conduct of weddings and funerals. Lines from a Judeo-Spanish (Ladino) love ballad of that period read, "Mother, if I should die, I don't want *chazanim* (cantors; singular, *chazan*) at my burial, but twelve young men, led by my beloved."[1]

In the 1920 play by H. Leivick (Leivick Halpern), *The Golem*, a 16th-century monster created by Rabbi Loewe of Prague to defend Jews against the infamous Blood Libel, slams shut the synagogue door. Afraid of its humanizing power, the *Golem* instinctively shuns *chazanut.*[2]

In his autobiography, *Main Leben*, Cantor Zavel Kwartin (1874–1953), quotes his father, who considered *chazanut*: "the highest honor we can bestow, to plead for the souls of fellow Jews." [3]

Up to recent times, one knew that the cantor's presence gave singing a prominence in traditional Jewish worship. As the title character said in Saul Bellow's novel, *Herzog*, "We'll live it up. We'll find an orthodox shul (synagogue) . . . enough of this Temple junk . . . we'll track down a good *chazan* . . . You and me, a pair of old-time Jews." [4]

Synagogue Song Today

Educator Steven Lorch notes that the traditional consumers of Synagogue song could produce it as well.[5] Worshippers preceded the cantor in reciting each paragraph, just as he summed up their collective effort before leading them into the next one. Celebrants of a shared rite, leader and followers had a common stock of musical ideas to build on. Singing breathed life into the service.

Now all that is changing. Many American cantors no longer lead a mutually recalled experience. How can they, when prayers are frequently read in unison English? Hebrew is increasingly limited to forced communal singing, often accompanied by noisy and abrupt hand-clapping, as if the congregation were a theater crowd dutifully applauding a play they did not understand. Without chant, Synagogue worship is a husk without its kernel.

In sum, we are no longer able to learn from live performance of *chazanut* in many American synagogues. Apart from English supplanting Hebrew and reading replacing recitative, Biblical chant, the motivic source of all Jewish music, is being relegated to an untutored laity. In abandoning the sounds to which congregations have always responded, contemporary American Jews deny to posterity the link to the past upon which the vitality of any folk depends.

Accessible Models of Chant

Trying to acquire the art of Synagogue song as a young cantor, I soon learned that conservatories offered little of relevance. So I sought for emulation the mature geniuses of New York's Orthodox synagogues, cantors like Berele Chagy (1892–1954), Moshe Koussevitsky (1899–1966), and Samuel Malavsky (1896–1985). Unfortunately, the old cantorial apprenticeship system was already *passé* at that time.

Eventually my zeal to discover the secrets of traditional *chazanut* led me to a manner of prayer-leading known as the Vienna *"Ritus."* This was originated by the legendary cantor Salomon Sulzer (1804–1890) in the 19th-century Dual-Monarchy formed by Austria and Hungary. Embracing elements of many ethnic subcultures, the Vienna *Ritus* had—by century's end—spread to the United States, where it flourished in Conservative synagogues until the end of World War II. I imbibed it in Baltimore's Chizuk Amuno Synagogue while assisting the venerable chazan, Abba Yosef Weisgal (1885–1981).

The well-ordered yet emotionally-charged Vienna approach has much to teach us about reverence and passion within a culturally pluralistic society. Once widely imitated as the modern embodiment of an ancient tradition, it knit Jewry together by abolishing time and place, turning those divided by history into contemporaries, and those separated by geography into neighbors.

What This Book Offers

To recapture the art of Synagogue song we must first isolate its basic components, four in all.

Psalmodic technique (**PART I** of this book), or reciting prayer-texts as diaspora communities have always chanted the Book of Psalms, is the oldest component of Synagogue song. Biblical technique, sometimes called cantillation (**PART II**), is the second oldest component. The third component, Modal technique, also called *nusach* (**PART III**), combines Psalmodic phraseology and Biblical motifs into prescribed ways of offering prayer for every liturgical occasion. The fourth component, Performance technique (**PART IV**), includes the various alterations that diaspora communities have made to the first three components, according to the prevalent usage of their host-cultures. It also includes combinations of the first three components, in life-cycle situations, for the reader to try.

The back of the book contains three working Appendices (**PART V**) plus an Index (PART VI). Appendix A defines 150 Hebrew and technical terms which appear throughout the book. Appendix B charts 248 motifs used in Lithuanian-style Biblical chant (the tradition most heard in America). Appendix C catalogues 30 Occurrences, 67 Recurrences, and 54 Parallels of a 12th-century motif-group, *Misinai* Tunes, plus a bibliography.

The Purpose of this Book

My hope is to inspire by informing, a timely step toward preserving Judaism's sacred musical heritage. *Synagogue Song in America* gives American Jews, seeking their ethnic roots, the keys to their musical past and the tools for reviving it along contemporary lines. In it, music lovers in general will learn—through clearly labeled examples—the secrets of Synagogue song's power.

In addition to informing our lay readers—Jews and Gentiles alike—I hope in the following chapters to share with synagogue officiants the wonder and beauty of liturgical chant, which is common to every culture. May they begin once again to breathe the magic of traditional song into the liturgy!

Preface: Bibliography & Notes

1. MAMA, Si Yo: *Ladino Folk Songs,* New York, Collectors Guild record CGL 605 (1961), side two, band six.
2. LEIVICK, H.: "The Golem," *Great Yiddish Plays,* translated and edited by Joseph C. Landis, New York, Bantam (1966), scene VIII, pages 337–339.
3. KWARTIN, Zavel: *Main Leben,* Philadelphia, Kamerling (1952), page 181; translated by Joseph A. Levine.
4. BELLOW, Saul: *Herzog,* New York, Viking (1961), page 91.
5. LORCH, Steven Charles: *The Convergence of Jewish and Western Culture as Exemplified through Music,* New York, Columbia University (1977), page 147.

PART I

PSALMODIC TECHNIQUE

Chazanut combines the long singing phrase
*[melodic flourish] with recitation-note
[reciting-tone] . . . For each note, as many
words as possible are fitted as the context
of the text allows.*

Changing Conceptions of Chazanut, 1949
Adolph Katchko

CHAPTER ONE

Jerusalem of Old

The oldest element of Synagogue song is a technique which, although originally associated with the Book of Psalms, has come to mean the rendition of any prayer text in what we think was the ancient Levitical manner. I call the technique 'Psalmodic', by which I mean a linear chant designed to follow the parallelistic structure of all Psalm-verses, most Biblical verses cited in prayer, and many prayers themselves. Psalmodic technique is thus a binary (sometimes ternary) recitative balanced by introductory and concluding flourishes in each segment. It is the driving force behind Synagogue worship.

The synagogue—as an institution—did not exist at the time of the Patriarchs, Judges, Prophets, and Kings (–2000 to –600). It probably arose during the Judean exile in Babylon (–586 to–538), and was brought back to Judea with the Jewish repatriation under Cyrus, ruler of Persia from –599 to –529. Its musical practice then took root in the Land of Israel, and with this development begins the long history of Synagogue song.

This first chapter examines the evolution of Levitical singing in the rituals of the First and Second Temples (the millenium from –950 to 70), then explores its transfer, as Psalmodic technique, to diaspora synagogues after the final fall of Jerusalem in 70. It also shows how this component of Jewish sacred chant paralleled early Christian singing. Finally, it leaps ahead 1900 years to see if Psalmodic-style singing still survives in the worship of 20th-century American churches and synagogues.

First-temple Singing

II Chronicles' description of the First Temple's dedication under King Solomon shows that the Book of Psalms provided the earliest texts for Temple singing. The passage (5:13) bears quoting:

> and it was the duty of the trumpeters and singers to make
> themselves heard in unison in praise and thanksgiving to
> the Lord, and when the song was raised, with trumpets and
> cymbals and other musical instruments, in praise to the
> Lord, "For he is good, for his steadfast love endures forever,"
> [from Psalm 118:1] . . .

Shortly before Nebuchadnezzar razed the First Temple in −586, King Hezekiah "stationed the Levites in the House of the Lord with cymbals, harps, and lyres" (II Chronicles 29:25). As many as 128 cymbals (Ezra 2:41; 3:10) and 120 trumpets (II Chronicles 5:12) joined the choir that sang over the burnt offering. Even with that volume of instrumentation, the song appears to have "sung itself," [1] i.e., to have overriden all else. Psalmodic chant as we know it today is rarely sung so loudly. We must infer that Levitical singing in the First Temple represented an earlier, more vigorous style.

Second-temple Singing

During the period of the Second Temple (built in −516, destroyed by Titus in 70), the human voice continued to lead, with instruments sweetening the sound. [2] The word 'Psalmodic', in fact, takes its name from the Greek *psalmos*, or hymn, which derives from *psallein*, to pluck: thus singing against a stringed background. In the Second Temple mainly strings accompanied the Psalms; brass and percussion filled lulls in the singing. By 70, the initial profusion of trumpets and cymbals had shrunk to a pair each. [3]

The same Levitical choir that sang to stringed accompaniment over burnt offerings in the outdoor courtyard of the Temple also sang *A cappella* (unaccompanied) in the indoor Chamber of Hewn Stone, *Lishkat Hagazit*. This room housed the Great Sanhedrin, or High Court of Justice, and served as synagogue within the Second-temple complex. No similar prayer-hall had existed in the First Temple. Whether stationed outside or inside, the Second-temple choir seems to have chanted identical Psalms.

One Talmudic sage who had been a Levitical chorister, Joshua ben Hananiah, has left us an account of his musical activities at the end of the first century. During certain special Festival occasions, the choristers apparently had little time to do much else than sing:

> When we used to rejoice at the place of the Water-drawing
> [during the eight-day Festival of Sukkot, or Tabernacles],
> our eyes saw no sleep . . . The first hour [was occupied with]
> the daily Morning sacrifice; from there we proceeded to
> Morning prayer; from there [we proceeded] to the Additional
> sacrifice . . . then the Afternoon prayer, then the Evening
> sacrifice, and after that the rejoicing at the place of the
> Water-drawing [all night].[4]

Nature of Second-temple Song

What were the characteristics of Second-temple song? The Talmud states that it was performed by a choir of no less than 12 Levites.[5] The Spanish-Jewish codifier, Maimonides (Moses ben Maimon, 1135–1204), explains that the Levitical choir was supported by a nearby ensemble of string players.[6] The Psalms must have been sung softly, since an eyewitness reports that the Priestly sacrifices with which they were associated took place in "the most complete silence."[7] (This despite our expectation that, with the number of public and private sacrifices being offered simultaneously on holy days, the din might have been considerable).

Historian Alfred Sendrey notes that many of the Psalms have subtitles indicating instrumentation other than that featured in the Temple rites. For instance, *El-hanechilot* ('to winds') for Psalm 5, *Al-alamot Shir* ('a song upon "maidens," ' or high-pitched lyres) for Psalm 46, and *Al-machalat* ('a dance-song' to the pipes that accompanied circle-dances) for Psalm 53. Other Psalms have subtitles indicating what seem to be the names of then-popular folk songs. For instance, *Al-hagatit* ('after "The Gittite" ') for Psalm 8, *Al-mut Labein* ('after "The Son's Death" ') for Psalm 9, and *Al-ayelet Hashachar* ('after "The Morning Hind" ') for Psalm 22. Sendrey believes that the Psalms bearing these subtitles were sung to the well-known song melodies named by the subtitles.[8]

But Psalms differ from songs, which mostly depend on their music. For the Levitical choir, words were what counted. The salient themes which the words expressed—praise of the Creator, comfort for the sorrowing, and commendation of the righteous—had to be clearly articulated. Moreover, the paired half-verses that make up each binary verse of most Psalms (some verses are ternary or three-part) are "parallel structures in which an idea is immediately restated in different words," as explained by musicologist Richard Hoppin.[9] According to the Mishnah (Tamid 5.6), Levitical function was "to speak in song." This implies liturgical recitative or chant, rather than singing.

Whatever chant-melody is used must fit the odd (as opposed to 'even') proportion of each pair of half-verses. Simple observation confirms this uneven proportion. The ratio of the lengths of these paired half-verses establishes a so-called Golden Section, where the longer half-verse is to the shorter as the sum of the pair is to the longer. This proportion holds for complete Psalms as well. Psalm 1, for instance, creates a Golden Section of 8:5 = 13:8. Eight initial statements describing "the righteous" counter five answering statements concerning "the wicked." (And the eight initial statements, divided into five attributes and three rewards, themseves comprise a Golden Section of 5:3 = 8:5). Philosopher Hugo Norden, who is responsible for the preceding analysis, sees the principle of a Golden Section extending to all the arts.[10]

Applied to a single pair of half-verses, a Golden Section of 3:2 = 5:3 (which is typical) will necessitate a pause in the melody somewhat past its halfway point, for balance. Since Levitical texts varied from day to day, depending on the liturgy, patterns for chanting Psalm-verses had to be flexible. The simplest solution would be a linear syllabic recitation followed by a melodic turn, repeated or varied for each pair of half-verses. To illustrate, EXAMPLE 1.1[11] shows a Golden Section from the concluding verse of Kiddush, the wine-ceremony ushering in the weekly Day of Rest. As in non-metrical chant generally, a semi-bar line (|) signals the initial pulse of each phrase.

> *Baruch atah, adonai,*
> *mekadeish hashabbat*

> 'Blessed art thou, O Lord,
> Sanctifier of the Sabbath'.

EXAMPLE 1.1
Psalmodic Golden Section of 3:2 = 5:3.

Tone Density

The hallmark of Psalmodic technique is its flexibility, a steady intonation of syllables followed by a multi-toned flourish. This results in alternating tone densities of one note per syllable (syllabic density) with a limitless number of notes per syllable (melismatic density). The effect is arresting, like the cracking of a whip (EXAMPLE 1.2).[12]

> *Leha'avir gilulim min ha'arets*
> '[We hope for the time] when you will remove
> all abominations from the earth.'

EXAMPLE 1.2
Change of tone density within a Psalmodic phrase.

Psalmodic technique's shift from syllabic-to-melismatic tone density places the melodic climax near the end of each phrase where, like an uncoiled spring, its tendency is to snap back to its original position. The ensuing phrase is thus propelled forward into its linear-recitative portion, and so on. This whip-cracking pattern fits Alfred Sendrey's hypothesis that the 55 Psalms bearing the heading *Lamenatsei'ach* ('to the Leader') were performed antiphonally by a Levitical precentor and chorus, since the subject pronoun in these Psalms alternates "I" with "We."[13] The rapid juxtaposition of linear declamation and vertical flourish also represents the essence of solo chazanic singing: intoning; erupting; and returning; with choral or congregational support. Finally, the text-structure of Psalmodic-technique leads inevitably to a form of binary recitation which later generations have come to call Psalmody or more precisely, Psalm Tones (more on this in the next subsection). Professor Eric Werner uses the term 'Psalmody' to define the rendition of any text after the manner in which (we think) Psalms were sung.[14] I use 'Psalmodic technique' in the same sense, as a universal standard against which the phrasal arrangement of Synagogue song may be measured.

Reciting-Tones

For convenience, Psalmodic transcription often groups syllabic intonation on a single pitch, as an extended whole-note in rectangular form ($\blacksquare$), called a reciting-tone (EXAMPLE 1.3).[15]

> *Titkabeil tselotehon uva'utehon . . .*
> 'May Israel's prayers be accepted by their
> Father who is in heaven'.

Tit-ka-beil tse-lo-te-hon uva'utehon dechol beit yisra'eil kodam avuhon di vishmaya ve'im-ru a-mein.

EXAMPLE 1.3
Reciting-tone: syllabic intonation grouped as an extended whole-note.

The reciting-tone appears again in the second half of each verse, but frequently with a different ending. Through lowering or raising the singing voice at the ends of phrases (just as is done with the speaking voice oratorically), Psalmodic technique divides its musical phrases into 'question-and-answer'. EXAMPLE 1.4[16] (after Deuteronomy 32:4) shows this:

> *Hatsur, tamim po'olo . . .*
> 'The Rock, his work is perfect;
> who shall dare question him?'

'question' 'answer'

Ha - tsur, tamim bechol ma-a-seh; mi yomar lo: mah ta - a-seh.
(reciting-tone)   (reciting tone)

EXAMPLE 1.4
Psalmodic reciting-tones, followed by different endings,
form musical 'question' and 'answer'.

Each reciting-tone is flanked by an ascending and/or a descending motif. EXAMPLE 1.5a shows the initial verse of Psalm 81, as chanted by the Jews of Iran, conventionally notated.[17] EXAMPLE 1.5b shows the same chant notated with reciting-tones.

> *Harninu leilohim uzeinu . . .*
> 'Sing aloud to God our strength;
> shout for joy to the God of Jacob'.

EXAMPLES 1.5c and 1.5d similarly show two ways of transcribing a chant from the Psalmodic repertory of the Roman Catholic Church (Psalm 95:1),[18] sung during the daily morning Office to the sixth of eight patterns known as Psalm Tones:

> *Venite, Exultemus Domino*
> 'O come, let us sing unto the Lord'.

EXAMPLE 1.5
Paired phrases, notated conventionally (a & c), and Psalmodically (b & d).

Although the Sixth Psalm-Tone's pattern (Example 1.5c) may resemble the Iranian Jew's Psalm-81 chant (Example 1.5a), its purpose here is to show Psalmodic transcription, and not to equate Church and Synagogue melodies. The truth is that both synagogue and church—at the beginning of the first millenium—shared a common Middle Eastern heritage, whose most highly stylized form of singing was evidently practiced in the Second Jerusalem Temple. From that noble repertoire both institutions borrowed certain elements, developing them along divergent lines.

From Temple to Synagogue

Prayer had long coexisted with animal sacrifice in ancient Israel. But even in −730 the prophet Hosea foresaw that, instead of offering bullocks, "we will render the fruit of our lips" (14:2). That prophecy came to pass when Nebuchadnezzar razed the First Temple in −586, and took the population captive to Babylon. With Jerusalem in ruins and the Temple gone, Jews refused to offer sacrifices in a foreign land, substituting verbal offerings in the form of prayers.

Most of the 42,360 Judean exiles who chose to return (including 200 male and female singers, according to Ezra 2:64-65) were repatriated about −550. They brought with them their prayers, by then organized into a formal service. Assembly halls to accommodate prayer services, known as synagogues (from the Greek *synagein*, 'to bring together'), sprang up throughout the 24 provinces of Judea. The Temple was rebuilt, and the reinstituted Daily sacrifice democratized through an institution called *Anshei Ma'amad*, or 'Standing Delegates'. Every province sent a delegation to Jerusalem twice yearly for a week of participation in Temple activities.

Since not all members of the delegation could make every journey, the ones who stayed home gathered in their local synagogue during the days they were supposed to be in the capital. The composition of this group corresponded to that of the group in Jerusalem. That is, it included the same proportion of Priests, Levites, and Israelites, and recited the same daily Psalms and other Bible readings at the times fixed for the obligatory offerings.[19] Talmudist Solomon Zeitlin suggests that the delegates who met in the outlying districts duplicated all aspects of the service held in the Temple's synagogue, the Chamber of Hewn Stone.[20]

Yet it is unlikely that more than one individual in any group of delegates would acquire sufficient skill and knowledge—during a biannual weekly visit—to lead a service back home. If the Levitical tradition of *A cappella* Psalmodic-style singing did spread to the 24 districts of Judea, it was probably in a solo version, and marked the beginning of the office of synagogue cantor as we know it.

Psalmodic Chant Enters the Church

Following Roman destruction of the Second Temple in the year 70, the intoning of prayer by a cantor—using Psalmodic technique in alternation with a responding congregation—persisted through the long exile. It was at the beginning of this period that early Christianity adopted the technique as the oldest stratum of Church singing.[21]

This is illustrated by the following Jewish and Christian texts. Following are nine lines from the Book of Psalms.

> How great art thy works, O Lord (92:5)
> Who is mighty as thou art, O Lord (89:8)
> The Lord is just in all his ways (145:17)
> O Lord, forevermore (93:5)
> A God feared in the council of the holy ones (89:7)
> And I will glorify thy name (86:12)
> Thou alone art God (86:10)
> All the nations . . .
> shall come and bow down before thee(86:9)
> Thy judgements are right (119:75)

Their appearance in the Book of Revelation (15:3–4), as shown below, supports historian Carl Kraeling's claim that Psalmodic statements were adapted by the Christian Bible.[22]

> 3. Great and wonderful are thy deeds,
> O Lord God the Almighty!
> Just and true are thy ways, O King of the Ages!
> 4. Who shall not fear and glorify thy name,
> O Lord, for thou alone art holy. All nations shall come and
> worship thee, for thy judgements have been revealed.

If the Church Fathers used Hebrew texts so openly, might they not also have imitated already-established patterns for the musical renditions of those texts? Clearly, the early Church Fathers were originally Jews, and would have used the music they knew. EXAMPLE 1.6a[23] cites a Balkan-Jewish confessional, quoting Psalm 47:5.

> *Alah elohim bitru'ah . . .*
> 'God has gone up with a shout;
> the Lord with the sound of a trumpet'.

Compare it to EXAMPLE 1.6b,[24] a Roman Catholic Invitatory on the Second Tone, quoting Psalm 148:1.

Laudate Dominum de coelis . . .
'Praise the Lord from the heavens;
praise him in the heights'.

EXAMPLE 1.6
Psalmodic chant in Synagogue and Church.

Examples 1.6a and 1.6b are only two of many, demonstrating that Psalmodic technique provided the foundation for Church as well as Synagogue singing in the early years of the first millenium.

Psalmodic Chant in Twentieth-century America

As I shall explain in **PART IV (PERFORMANCE TECHNIQUE: The Americanization of Synagogue Song)**, a uniform style of worship cuts across all denominational lines in Twentieth-century America. This is evident in the United States Government's *Song and Service Book* for the armed forces; the 'official' worship style features communal reading punctuated by communal singing. EXAMPLE 1.7a offers three governmentally recommended hymns for: Protestant (EXAMPLE 1.7a, "Old Hundredth");[25] Catholic (EXAMPLE 1.7b, "Blessed Sacrament");[26] and Jewish services (EXAMPLE 1.7c, *Ein Keiloheinu* ['None is like Our God, none like our Lord, none like our King, none like our Redeemer']).[27]

Intended for congregational participation, the three hymns of Example 1.7 evenly divide their eight-measure periods into symmetrical phrases. They are all sung in four-part harmony, to common time ($\frac{4}{4}$). Their tone density is almost exclusively syllabic, avoiding both the reciting-tones and melismatic flourishes of Psalmodic technique.

EXAMPLE 1.7

Uniform singing-style in American churches and synagogues: symmetrical
phrases; four-part harmony; common time; syllabic tone density.

The worship format of Twentieth-century America was described as far back as 1851:

> The one who presides stands on a high place holding his book. He asks [those attending] to open their books to certain places; then they all read together; then they listen to his explanation; and then they all leave together.[28]

Originally Protestant, rote-reading—followed by commentary—with periodic hymn singing, is now the norm for Reform and Conservative Jewish services as well. If the flexibility and sweep of (supposed) Levitical style finds any vestige in Twentieth-century American worship, it is through the solo chant of traditional cantors. The ensuing chapter surveys the appearance (and disappearance) of this Psalmodic vestige throughout the yearly cycle of American Synagogue song.

Jerusalem Of Old: Bibliography & Notes

1. KIMCHI, David: Commentary on II Chronicles 29:28; contrary to most translations, the Hebrew is reflexive, and demands this rendering.
2. TALMUD: Babylonian, Sukkah 51a.
3. MISHNAH: Tamid 7.3.
4. TALMUD: Babylonian, Sukkah 53a, translated from the Aramaic by I. Epstein, London, Soncino (1938), volume III, page 225.
5. MISHNAH: Arakhin 2.6.
6. MAIMONIDES: *Mishneh Torah*, Sefer Avodah, K'lei Hamikdash 3:3.
7. ARISTEAS, Letter of: Translated from the Greek by Herbert T. Andrews, *The Apocrypha and Pseudepigrapha of the Old Testament in English*, edited by R.H. Charles, Oxford, Clarendon (1966), Volume II, verse 95.
8. SENDREY, Alfred: *Music in Ancient Israel*, New York, Philosophical (1969), pages 120; 130.
9. HOPPIN, Richard H.: *Medieval Music*, New York, Norton (1978), page 81.
10. NORDEN, Hugo: *Form—The Silent Language*, Boston, Branden (1968), throughout the book, calling the Golden Section "a principle of 'Dynamic Symmetry'."
11. KIDDUSH: *Liturgie Sephardie*, edited by O. Camhy, London, World Sephardi Federation (1959), adapted from page 24.
12. KWARTIN, Zevulun: *Smiroth Zebulon*, New York, published by the author (1938), number 41.

13. SENDREY (see item 8), pages 114–117; for instance, Psalms 5, 9, 18, 31, 41, 46, 47, 59, 62, 70, 75, etc.
14. WERNER, Eric: *The Sacred Bridge*, New York, Columbia (1959), page 26, superseding his earlier designation of Psalmody as "a musical rendition of sacred texts in public worship." (See "Preliminary Notes for a Comparative Study of Catholic and Jewish Musical Punctuation," in *Hebrew Union College Annual*, Cincinnati, Volume XV (1940), p. 335).
15. LEVINE, Joseph A.: *Emunat Abba* (Baltimore Hebrew College, 1981), Ann Arbor, University Microfilms, Volume I, number 219.
16. SULZER, Salomon: *Schir Zion*, (Vienna, 1839–1865), revised by Joseph Sulzer, Vienna, (1905), number 478.
17. IDELSOHN, Abraham Zvi: *Toledot Haneginah Ha'ivrit*, Tel Aviv, Dvir (1924), page 233.
18. BRIGGS, H.B., and W.H. Frere: *Manual of Plainsong*, London, Novello (1902), page 21.
19. TALMUD: Babylonian, Berachot 26b. TOSEFTA: Berachot 3.1. MISHNAH: Ta'anit 4.2 (Bertinoro's commentary). MAIMONIDES: *Mishneh Torah*, Sefer Avoda 6.2.
20. ZEITLIN, Solomon: "The Origin of the Synagogue," *Proceedings of the American Academy for Jewish Research* (1931), page 78.
21. WAGNER, Peter: "Ursprung und Entwicklung der liturgischen Gesangformen," *Einführung in die gregorianischen Melodien*, Freiburg, Veith (1895), Volume I, pages 6–16.
22. KRAELING, Carl H.: "Music in the Bible," *New History of Music*, Volume I, edited by Egon Wellesz, Oxford, Clarendon (1957), page 304.
23. IDELSOHN (see item 12), page 279.
24. IDELSOHN (see item 12), page 239.
25. OLD HUNDREDTH: *Song and Service Book for Ship and Field*, edited by Ivan L. Bennet, Washington, DC, United States Government Printing Office (1942), page 5.
26. BLESSED SACRAMENT (see item 23), page 67, number 45.
27. EIN KEILOHEINU (see item 23), page 74.
28. HOUCHINS, Lee: *Abroad in America*, edited by Marc Pachter and Frances Wein, Reading, MA, Addison-Wesley (1976), page 100.

CHAPTER TWO

Climbing the Liturgical Ladder

Synagogue song increases in complexity—as does Synagogue liturgy—on Sabbaths and during the Pilgrimage Festivals of Pesach (Passover), Shavuot (Pentecost), and Sukkot (Tabernacles). It takes its most elaborate form on the High Holy Days of Rosh Hashanah (New Year) and Yom Kippur (Day of Atonement).

On each ascending rung of this liturgical ladder, special prayers are added: Sabbath *piyyutim* (laudatory poems); Festival Psalms; High Holy Day *selichot* (penitential laments). All of these insertions require treatment commensurate with their importance; the 'higher' the moment, the more embellished the performance.

Surrounded by this increasing complexity, Psalmodic technique persists. It introduces and concludes choral settings, signals congregational responses, and provides a recitation medium for the many *Keva* (Statutory) prayers that recur in every service. This chapter looks at Weekday song and then explores the adjustments which Psalmodic technique makes in order to fit the heightened mood of Sabbaths, Festivals, and High Holy Days.

Weekday Song

Psalmodic technique forms the bedrock of Weekday song, in the morning (Shacharit), afternoon (Minchah), and evening (Maariv) services. In Orthodox American synagogues workaday Shacharit occurs between 6–8 a.m.; the Code of Law (*Shulchan Aruch*) forbids having breakfast or doing business beforehand.[1] Minchah starts 15 minutes before sunset; Maariv begins shortly thereafter, following a brief session of Talmud study.

Both cantor (often a lay person) and congregation (often only a Minyan, or quorum of ten adults) need to hurry Weekday worship—within the time-frames—so that they can get to work or supper. Rapid, unadorned chant-formulas are required; typical of these is the Weekday Kedushah ('Sanctification') prayer (EXAMPLE 2.1).[2]

Example 2.1 reveals one variation of plain Psalmodic technique: while the syllabic recitation is really on one note (A♭) throughout, it rises to its upper neighbor (B♭) at every stressed syllable (indicated by a musical accent >). The Kedushah-chant for Shacharit or Minchah is most representative of weekday song.

> *Nekadeish et shimcha ba'olam . . .*
> 'We sanctify thy name in the world
> even as they sanctify it in heaven. . .
> as written by thy prophet. And they
> called one unto the other, and said':

EXAMPLE 2.1
Opening and closing motifs of Weekday Kedushah
(for Shacharit or Minchah).

Sabbath Song

With Sabbath song we move up a rung on the ladder, in terms of complexity. An excerpt from the Shabbat (Sabbath) Morning liturgy called *Pesukei Dezimra*, or 'Passages of Song', shows the rising stressed syllables. The reciting-tones of each of the verse's paired phrases rise as well (EXAMPLE 2.2).[3]

> *Vehu kechatan yotsei meichupato . . .*
> 'The sun, which comes forth like a
> bridegroom leaving his chamber, and like a
> strong man runs its course with joy'
> (Psalm 19:5).

EXAMPLE 2.2
Sabbath Morning *Pesukei Dezimra.*

Another Sabbath variation appears in Psalm 95—*Lechu Neranenah*—recited during the Friday Night service of Sabbath welcome, *Kabbalat Shabbat* (EXAMPLE 2.3).[4]

> 1. O come, let us sing to the Lord;
> let us make a joyful noise
> to the rock of our salvation.
> 2. Let us come into his presence
> with thanksgiving;
> let us make a joyful noise to him
> with songs of praise!
> 3. For the Lord is a great God;
> and a great King above all gods.
> 4. In his hand are the depths of the earth;
> the heights of the mountains are his also.

In this responsive style—typical of German-Jewish, or Western European usage—almost every verse is sung at a different pitch. Note how the cantor's and congregation's alternate verses as well as reciting-tones vary:

<u>Cantor:</u>	verse 1 on <u>F</u>
<u>Congregation:</u>	verse 2 on <u>F</u> and <u>E</u>
<u>Cantor:</u>	verse 3 on <u>A</u> and <u>G</u>
<u>Congregation:</u>	verse 4 on <u>C</u> and <u>A</u>

EXAMPLE 2.3
Friday Night *Kabbalat Shabbat* (Western European style).

Renderings of Psalm 95 for *Kabbalat Shabbat* vary. EXAMPLE 2.4[5] illustrates a recitation-style practiced in the Eastern European synagogues of Poland, Russia, and the Balkan countries. It differs in three ways from the previous example. First, a solo cantor picks up the text almost at its conclusion, from verse 10, after the congregation's prior reading of the entire Psalm. The cantor continues to the end, leading the congregation into the ensuing prayer, Psalm 96. Example 2.4 shows only the first phrase of verse 10:

Arba'im shanah akut bedor
'For forty years I loathed that generation'.

The second way Eastern European *Kabbalat Shabbat* chant differs from its Western counterpart is in its brilliantly florid style that avoids the reciting-tone and removes all sense of the Psalm's paired phrases.

The third way it differs is in its use of vocal ornamentation to "teach" the text. The word *arba'im* ('forty') appears in Example 2.4 three times. The first time, its rising ornamentation seems to create a feeling of optimism, the second time a feeling of longing, and the third time a feeling of finality. These three ways of rendering the word *arba'im* dramatize God's hope for, disappointment with, and loathing for the people he had delivered from bondage. A mirror-sequence occurs on the word *akut* ('I loathed'), interpreting musically the subsiding of God's wrath in three stages: regret; divine struggle; and resignation.

Because Eastern European style introduced ornamentation, perhaps to excess, it met opposition upon spreading from Poland to Germany after the Chmielnicki persecutions of 1648–1658. Western European rabbis opposed the new Eastern style because it consumed so much time in the *Kabbalat Shabbat* section of Friday Night worship that later prayers (Maariv proper) had to be rushed. Resenting this intrusion on the sedate Western norm, Rhineland rabbis soon restricted the number of Eastern-style renditions that cantors were allowed to feature.[6]

EXAMPLE 2.4
Friday Night *Kabbalat Shabbat* (Eastern European style).

A compromise that would eventually satisfy East and West evolved in the Vienna *Ritus*, an approach that merged Eastern pyrotechnics with Western dignity. It was popularized by the great 19th-century cantor, Salomon Sulzer, whose monumental collection, *Schir Zion* (1839–1865), became a sourcebook for hundreds of disciples. Abba Weisgal (1885–1981), one of the last American exponents of this style, brought the *Ritus* to Baltimore in 1920. EXAMPLE 2.5[7] is my transcription of Weisgal's Psalm 95 for *Kabbalat Shabbat*, verses 3–9 (i.e., the cantor's part only).

> 3. For the Lord is a great God,
> and a great King above all gods.
> 5.The sea is his, for he made it;
> for his hands formed the dry land.
> 7. For he is our God,
> and we are the people of his pasture,
> and the sheep of his hand.
> O that today you would hearken to his voice!
> 9. When your fathers tested me,
> and put me to the proof, though they had seen my work.

EXAMPLE 2.5
Vienna-*Ritus* compromise for Friday Night *Kabbalat Shabbat*.

This Vienna-*Ritus* compromise for *Kabbalat Shabbat* conforms to Western practice, with cantor and congregation both chanting on reciting-tones. The cantor's statements are more florid yet strictly within the limits of Psalmodic form. The congregation responds on pitches signaled by the cantor. Melodic flourishes burgeon but word-repetition is avoided. The balance between every pair of phrases is maintained.

Festival Song

Just as in the case of Sabbath song, regional variations have determined the ways of rendering prayers Psalmodically on the Pilgrimage Festivals that coincide with the advent of spring, summer, and fall in the Land of Israel. We will look at both Western and Eastern European examples.

Psalms 113–118, called Psalms of Praise, or Hallel, are added to the Festival Shacharit liturgy, and for them German cantors used the call-and-response format already observed in *Kabbalat Shabbat* (Example 2.3). The form originated with the Song at the Sea in Exodus 15 (verses 1–21). The Talmud says,"Moses intoned the first verse; the Israelites responded with the second verse, Moses intoned the third verse; etc."[8] Jacketed in rigid $\frac{4}{4}$ meter, 19th-century German-Jewish renditions of the Hallel Psalms—even using this ancient responsive format—resembled marching-songs.

EXAMPLE 2.6 [9] samples a German formula for reciting all of Hallel. We show the setting for Psalm 113, verses 1 and 2:

> ... *halelu avdei adonai* ...

> 1. '[Praise the Lord!]'
> Praise, O servants of the Lord,
> praise the name of the Lord!
> 2. Blessed be the name of the Lord
> from this time forth and for evermore!

The composer Louis Lewandowsky (1821–1894) describes the marching song pattern of Example 2.6 as "Psalmody," to be performed by cantor and congregation "verse by verse." [10] Since Lewandowsky was Sulzer's counterpart in Berlin, we can be sure this adaptation of Psalmodic chant was widely imitated by German-speaking communities west of the Austro-Hungarian empire. It shows how far Synagogue song had strayed from its Levitical origins in some parts of Europe by 1871.

CANTOR

1. Ha - le - lu, av - dei — a -do-nai, ha - le - lu —— et sheim a - do - nai. ——

CHOIR AND CONGREGATION

2. Yehi sheim a - do - nai mevo - rach. mei - a - tah ve'ad o - lam.

EXAMPLE 2.6
German Marching-song formula for Festival Hallel.

The departure is felt even more keenly since the opening six paragraphs of Hallel (Psalms 113–116) are traditionally conceived in a more flexible manner, metrical tunes being welcomed by all European traditions only in the closing six paragraphs (Psalms 117–118).

Eastern European cantors, meanwhile, use rigidity in a different way. EXAMPLE 2.7[11] renders a verse from another Hallel Psalm (118:18).

> *Yasor yisrani yah . . .*
> 'The Lord has chastened me sorely, but he
> has not given me over to death'.

A recitative written almost 100 years after Lewandowsky's march, Example 2.7 cramps the Biblical Hebrew into triplicate $\frac{3}{4}$ meter. Its Russian-born composer, Israel Alter (1901–1979), spoke Yiddish, and set the Psalm to the speech inflection with which he was most familiar. In Yiddish the main poetic foot is a dactyl, two unstressed syllables following a stressed syllable.

> *| Sho–lem a– | lei–chem, reb | Al–ter? _ |*

> | 'How do you | do, Mis–ter | Al–ter?'_ |

Psalm 118:18

Ya - sor yis-rani yah, ve-la-ma-vet; ve-la-ma-vet lo; —— lo, —— lo ——— ne-ta-na - ni.
　　　1　　　　2　　　　3　　　　4　　　5　　　6　　　7　　　　8

EXAMPLE 2.7
Dactylic speech-pattern for Festival Hallel.

In Example 2.7, notice how, on the first staff, the dactylic rhythm of the words (stress-off-off) coincides with the triple-meter of the music. With the second staff, the rhythm of the words oversteps bar-lines as it moves to its own beat. Measures 4 and 5 lose a beat in the process; measures 5, 6, 7, and 8 shift their accents from the first to the final beat.

The dactylic rhythms and meters of Examples 2.6 and 2.7 are far from typical Hebrew versification. In Hebrew the main poetic foot is an anapest, two unstressed syllables preceding a stressed syllable, the reverse image of the dactyl.

Mah nish- / mah ba-o- / lam, a-do- / ni?

'What is I new in the I world, my good I man?'

Anapestic rhythm opens up the possibility of a Psalmodic alternative to the German $^4_4$ rigidity and Russian $^3_4$ rigidity seen in Examples 2.6 and 2.7. Look at the stress-pattern of Psalm 118:5:

min ha– / mei–tsar karati / yah,
'Out of my dis– I tress I called on the I Lord,

__a– / na–ni va– / mer – chav / yah
__the I Lord __ I an– swered I me.'

EXAMPLE 2.8a[12] sets it to music, in $^2_4$ time, to show how the anapestic stresses can be notated conventionally. EXAMPLE 2.8b transcribes the same setting with reciting-tones, to show how the Psalmodic alternative offers freedom of expression to performers.

Psalm 118:24

EXAMPLE 2.8
Anapestic speech-pattern for Festival Hallel.

High Holy Day Song

We now arrive at the summit of Synagogue song, the solemn observances of Rosh Hashanah and Yom Kippur. Generations of cantor-composers have provided the High Holy Day liturgy with what Salo Baron calls "running poetic commentary."[13] In order to make time for congregational hymns, parts of this rich layer of Biblical imagery are often omitted in today's American synagogues. Often omitted as well are many *Keva* (Statutory) prayers. Yet *Keva* prayers form the backbone of every service, providing structure and pace. The 'entry'-prayer, *Hamelech* ('The King!'), for instance, heralds the approach of the morning Declaration of Faith (Shema), and of the Shacharit Standing Devotion (*Amidah*). The musical genre of *Hamelech* is that of a fanfare; cantors use it to announce themes that will figure later in the service. Compare the simplicity of chanting *Hamelech* on the Sabbath (EXAMPLE 2.9a)[14] with the complexity of chanting it on High Holy Days EXAMPLE 2.9b).[15] On High Holy Days it consists almost entirely of coloratura (melismatic flourishes).

Hamelech, hayosheiv al kisei ram venisa
'The King! The One who sits upon a high and lofty throne'.

EXAMPLE 2.9
Simple and Complex versions of *Hamelech*.

Statutory prayers all receive more florid treatment on High Holy
Days than they do on Festivals, Sabbaths, or weekdays. (*Hamelech*, inci-
dentally, doesn't even appear on weekdays). Compare the straightforward closing motif of Weekday Kedushah (Example 2.1b) with its
drawn-out counterpart in High Holy Day Kedushah (EXAMPLE 2.10):[16]

kakatuv al-yad nevi'echa . . .
'as written by thy prophet' (see Example 2.1b).

(For Shacharit/Minchah/Neilah)

EXAMPLE 2.10
High Holy Day Kedushah: closing motif.

How, then, does the basic Psalmodic formula (syllabic intonation
flanked by melismatic flourishes) fit the High Holy Day liturgy? With
difficulty, as we shall see; mostly as bridge-passages. A transitional
bridge analogous to the *Hamelech* Introit-fanfare of Example 2.9b, for
instance, appears in the Rosh Hashanah Musaf ('Additional') service.

Ve'et musaf yom hazikaron hazeh . . .
'and the Musaf Offering of this Day of
Remembrance we will prepare and offer to
you in love'.

Music of the cantor-composer, Salomon Weintraub (1721–1829), is
more rhapsodic than Psalmodic (EXAMPLE 2.11a).[17] Compare
Weintraub's rhapsodic *Ve'et Musaf* with my transcription of a Psalmodic
version (EXAMPLE 2.11b).[18] Observe how the Psalmodic bridge saves
time (about seven-and-a-half seconds versus fifteen seconds for Example
2.11a) while maintaining a devotional mood.

EXAMPLE 2.11
Rosh Hashanah Musaf: bridge-passage treatments.

Summing Up

Readers may have perceived by now the underlying rationale for chanting on reciting-tones; they represent the quickest means of getting where we are going—in the text—through music. While not a panacea, this part of Psalmodic technique enables even a novice to lead prayer services, so long as he or she can articulate Hebrew words.

As demonstration, we will consider Judaism's Declaration of Faith:

> *Shema, yisra'eil:*
> *adonai eloheinu, adonai echad*

> 'Hear, O Israel:
> The Lord our God is one Lord'
> (Deuteronomy 6:4).

EXAMPLE 2.12 sets it on four rungs of the liturgical ladder, using syllabic reciting-tone intonation in four of the five versions. Note the increasing complexity at the end of each phrase, as we ascend from weekday to Sabbath to Festival to High Holy Day.

EXAMPLE 2.12a places the Declaration of Faith (sometimes called simply, Shema) in Weekday prayer, using the pattern given in Example 2.1a. EXAMPLE 2.12b adds a bit of drama—in the *Kabbalat Shabbat* style of Example 2.5, verses 7 and 9. EXAMPLE 2.12c tries its hand at the Yiddish-inflected dactylic pattern of Example 2.7. EXAMPLE 2.12d reverts to a simpler line, imitating the Hebrew-inflected anapestic pattern of Example 2.8. Our *pièce de résistance* is EXAMPLE 2.12e, a Psalmodic adaptation of the *Hamelech*-fanfare in Example 2.9b.

EXAMPLE 2.12
The Shema, set Psalmodically and otherwise.

The Congregational 'Drone'

Congregational "repeats" are traditional whenever the Shema is sung; they are inseparable from Psalmodic technique, growing out of the reciting-tones. That is why our single non-psalmodic setting, Example 2.12c, will not work; it contains no reciting-tone for the congregation to recall and repeat.

Syllabic recitation can now be seen as the force behind Synagogue prayer, a generator of energy linking the one who leads with those being led. If Psalmodic chant is performed effectively, worshippers will not only respond on cue, but also will move along with the cantor's line in an undertone. This constant 'drone' has become recognized as an organic part of Synagogue prayer, sometimes in a negative sense, due to its formlessness.[19]

Yet in the context of Synagogue song, the 'drone' has always characterized the coordinated effort of cantor and congregation, a vocal continuum that does not abate during the course of worship. It ceases only with the final phrase, whether of Weekday, Sabbath, or High Holy Day prayer. The switch that activates this tonal current has remained: the near-electric sound of Psalmodic chant.

Climbing the Liturgical Ladder: Bibliography & Notes

1. KITSUR SHULCHAN ARUCH: VIII 1–2.
2. LEVINE, Joseph A.: *Emunat Abba* (Baltimore Hebrew College, 1981), Ann Arbor, University Microfilms, Volume I, number 80.
3. LACHMANN, Isaak: *Awaudas Jisroeil*, Leipzig, Roeder (1899), number 154.
4. JAPHET, Israel Mayer: *Schirei Jeschurun*, Frankfurt, Kaufmann (1881), number 3.
5. KWARTIN, Zevulun: *Smiroth Zebulon*, New York, published by the author (1928), number 1.
6. IDELSOHN, Abraham Zvi: "Songs and Singers of the Synagogue in the Eighteenth Century," *Hebrew Union College Jubilee Volume*, Cincinnati (1925), page 405.
7. LEVINE (see item 2), Volume II, number 254.
8. MISHNAH: Sukkah 3.9–11.
9. LEWANDOWSKY, Louis: *Kol Rinnah U't'fillah*, Berlin, published by the author (1871), number 78.
10. LEWANDOWSKY (see item 9), number 78, below.
11. ALTER, Israel: *Cantorial Recitatives for Hallel, Tal and Geshem*, New York, School of Sacred Music (1962), pages 14–15.
12. LEVINE (see item 2), Volume II, number 423.
13. BARON, Salo Wittmayer: *A Social and Religious History of the Jews*, Philadelphia, Jewish Publication Society (1958), Volume VII, page 97.
14. BAER, Abraham: *Baal T'fillah*, Gothenburg, published by the author (1877), numbers 488a–489a.
15. BAER (see item 17), adapted from numbers 1002-1008.
16. BAER (see item 17), number 1108b.
17. WEINTRAUB, Hirsch: *Schire Beth Adonai*, Koenigsburg, published by the author (1859–1861), Volume III (Compositions of his father, Salomon Weintraub), number 197.
18. LEVINE (see item 2), Volume I, number 61.
19. BANCHIERI, Adriano: *Pazzia Senile* ('Aged Folly', a comic opera, 1598); and *La Sinogoga* ('The Synagogue', a madrigal, 1623); in both of which the 'drone' is caricatured musically.
20. BACHMANN, Jacob: *Schirath Jacob*, Odessa, Jurgenson (1884), number 17.
21. FRIEDMANN, Aron: *Schir Lisch'laumau*, Berlin, Deutsche-Israelitischen Gemeindebunde (1901), number 398a.
22. HELLER, Josef: *Kol T'hilloh*, Brno, Winiker (1914), Volume II, number 260.
23. SULZER (see item 4), number 410b.
24. LEVINE (see item 2), Volume I, number 160c.
25. NAUMBOURG, Samuel: *Zemirot Yisraeil*, Paris, published by the author (1847), number 264b.
26. IDELSOHN (see item 6), page 282:a.

PART II

BIBLICAL TECHNIQUE

In our hands are a number of motifs—
a tradition—passed from generation
to generation . . . at whose appearance in the
old Prayer chant worshippers tremble . . .
And if this is true for prayer,
how much more so for Biblical chant.

Tselilei Hamikra, 1955
Yehoshua Leib Ne'eman

CHAPTER
THREE

Tone Density; Neumes; *Misinai* Tunes

In this chapter we define Biblical technique by comparing its tone density and pace to that of Psalmodic technique. We analyze its characteristic figurations (neume motifs), observe the way they are sung in various diaspora communities (including the United States), and show how they spawned one group of prayer motifs reverently called *Nigunei Misinai* ('Tunes from Mount Sinai').

Tone Density

Synagogue song, in all its chant-forms—Psalmodic, Biblical, or Modal— draws its motifs from the musical reading of Hebrew Scripture, a practice at least 2,500 years old.[1] When performed from handwritten scrolls devoid of vowels or punctuation, Biblical technique depends for its effect as much on rhetoric as it does on melody.

Since the late-18th century, some writers have applied to Scripture reading (from which practice I extract the characteristic note-grouping as 'Biblical technique') the name, cantillation (from the Latin *cantillare*, 'sing low'). Others have lately used "cantillation" to describe the patterned recitation of liturgical texts generally, including Psalms.[2] This has led to confusion between three separate techniques: Psalmodic; Biblical; and Modal. All three of these techniques may be applied—singly or in combination—to any classic Hebrew text, whether a Psalm, a portion of Scripture, or a prayer. One purpose of this book is to show the differences between the three techniques as well as the ways in which they work best together.

In Psalmodic technique, which some scholars date earlier,[3] the sense of ebb and flow arises from a change in density of tones as the voice passes from one part of a phrase to another. The tone density of Biblical technique falls halfway between the Psalmodic extremes of one note per syllable (syllabic) to as many notes per syllable as breath will allow (melismatic). Two to five notes per syllable (neumatic) are typical of Biblical technique's tone density; this skirts the monotony of a reciting-tone while avoiding the exhaustion of endless ornamentation.

Treatments of a Friday Night Prayer motif, *Eil Chai Vekayam* ('O ever living God'), demonstrate the three tone densities. EXAMPLE 3.1a[4] by Salomon Sulzer of Vienna apportions one note to each syllable, through brevity implying a slow, sustained tempo. The *f* dynamic ensures that this sparse density will be sung with vigor.

a. Syllabic: *one note per syllable*

Eil   chai   ve-ka-yam,

b. Neumatic: *two to five notes per syllable*

Eil___ chai ve-ka-yam, ___

c. Melismatic: *many notes per syllable*

Eil   chai___ ve-ka-yam, ___

EXAMPLE 3.1
Three tone densities for a Prayer motif.

EXAMPLE 3.1b[5] by Israel Alter of the United States stretches two of three accented syllables into moderately paced figurations of two and five notes. This is the Biblical-technique approach. The lower vocal register suggests a dynamic of *mf*.

EXAMPLE 3.1c[6] by Aron Friedmann of Berlin reveals the greatest density, providing melismas (multi-toned syllables) of ten and seven notes. The quick shift from lower-middle to upper-middle to lower register demands no louder a dynamic than *mp*.

To more clearly demonstrate the differences between Psalmodic and Biblical techniques—both in density and pace—we will look at two versions of Jeremiah 31:20.

Havein yakir li efrayim . . .
'Is Ephraim my dear son?
is he my darling child?'

EXAMPLE 3.2a[7], virtuoso prayer-rendition for Rosh Hashanah by Sholom Katz of the United States, shows the Psalmodic pattern of rapid reciting-tone followed by equally rapid melisma. The tone densities of this phrase move from one note per syllable to 19 notes per syllable, yielding an average density of 10 notes per syllable.

Compare it to EXAMPLE 3.2b, a reconstruction of a Scripture-reading pattern popular in contemporary American synagogues. This pattern is based upon a Northern European tradition formalized in the Lithuanian capitol of Vilna during the 18th century, and later codified by Solomon Rosowsky (1878–1962). Example 3.2b, borrowing from Rosowsky's chart of Biblical neume motifs (see Appendix B),[8] has four motifs using neumatic groupings of four, two, five, and again five notes per syllable. Its average tone density is thus four, or 40 percent that of Psalmodic technique.

Readers may wish to explore the tempo and dynamic best suited to each Example. I would suggest that the Psalmodic pattern (Example 3.2a) last about five seconds at *mp*, the Biblical pattern (Example 3.2b) about nine seconds at *mf*.

Just as in Example 3.1, the operative principle is: greater tone density implies faster tempo and softer dynamic; lesser tone density implies slower tempo and louder dynamic. Psalmodic technique, with an average tone density of 10, is generally sung almost twice as fast and half as loud as Biblical technique, whose average tone density is four.

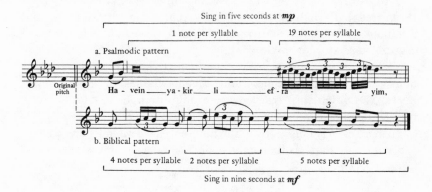

EXAMPLE 3.2
Comparing Psalmodic and Biblical patterns of tone density and pace.

Neumes

One reason for the difference in tempo and dynamics just discussed is that, unlike Psalmodic technique which reserves its motif for a single syllable toward the phrase-end, Biblical chant assigns a motif to each word. It does this with signs called *neumes* (*te'amim* in Hebrew). Rosowsky and others called *te'amim* "tropes" (after the Greek *tropos*, 'turn'), but this is misleading; trope has come to mean inserting a new text or melody within a traditional Gregorian chant.[9] Current understanding of neumes, however, fits the function of *te'amim* perfectly: symbols indicating the relative pitch (and rhythm) of various motifs.[10] (I caution the reader to bear in mind that neumes have meaning only to one trained in a particular tradition).

The second phrase of Exodus 31:16 will illustrate. It enjoins the Children of Israel to rest every seventh day,

> *la'asot et-hashabbat ledorotam*
> 'observing the Sabbath throughout
> their generations'.

EXAMPLE 3.3a quotes a chant using Psalmodic technique for this phrase.[11] It groups 19 notes on the final syllable.

EXAMPLE 3.3b renders the same text into Biblical chant for the Torah (the first five books of the Hebrew Bible) according to Rosowsky.[12]

The signs below the words are the neumes, indicating the motif assigned to each word. The motif transcribed above the word *et-hashabbat* ('the Sabbath') has eight notes. Going back to the initial word, *la'asot* ('observing'), its motif contains six notes, as does the motif above the final word, *ledorotam* ('throughout their generations'). Torah readers generally intone each word with equal emphasis. Psalmodic squeezing of several words onto one note—in order to expand the final syllable into a melismatic flourish—is foreign to Biblical technique.

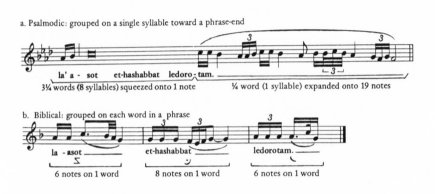

a. Psalmodic: grouped on a single syllable toward a phrase-end

la' a - sot   et-hashabbat   ledoro - tam.
3¼ words (8 syllables) squeezed onto 1 note   ¼ word (1 syllable) expanded onto 19 notes

b. Biblical: grouped on each word in a phrase

la - asot _____   et-hashabbat _____   ledorotam. _____
6 notes on 1 word   8 notes on 1 word   6 notes on 1 word

EXAMPLE 3.3
Grouping of motifs in Psalmodic and Biblical chant.

The root of "neume" in Hebrew, *ta'am* (singular of *te'amim*), has several meanings: 'taste'; 'accent'; 'sense'. Neumes impart taste (intonation) to Scripture through melody, accent through placement (above or below the stressed syllable), and sense (rhetoric) by their ability to create a pause or to run words together. In addition to these functions, neumes provide a means of memorizing the intonation, accentuation, and rhetoric of the handwritten scrolls read publicly, for only consonants appear on these scrolls. (Semitic languages are generally read without vowels, but accuracy is paramount in the case of Holy Writ). Vowels and punctuation—as well as neumes—appear only in *printed* editions of the Hebrew Bible.

The system of neumes used today dates from the early 10th-century school centered in the town of Tiberias, on the western shore of the Sea of Galilee. The Tiberian system, formulated by Aaron ben Moses ben Asher, was the first to use a sign to represent each of the 28 neumes, rather than alphabet letters or dots. It's the Tiberian system that appears in the 21 prose books of Hebrew Scripture. (The system appearing in the poetical books—Job, Proverbs, Psalms—represents motifs and word-groupings long forgotten.)[13]

Rosowsky divides the 28 neumes grammatically into six basic groups. Each group takes its name from its final neume, after which the reader is supposed to come to a full stop. Groups 3., 4., and 6. have a special neume (shown at the end of the group, in parentheses) which sometimes substitutes for the whole group.

Rosowsky calls seven of the neumes 'connectors': *mercha, munach, mahpach, darga, ketanah*, *kadma, yerach-ben-yomo.* A connector's motif and the motif that follows should be sung without the slightest pause.

The six neume groups

Number of group	Name of group	Name of neume
1.	SOF-PASUK	mercha tipcha | mercha sof-pasuk ‖
		Neume itself
2.	ETNACHTA	mercha tipcha | munach etnachta ‖
3.	SEGOL	munach zarka | munach segol** (shalshelet) ‖
4.	KATON	mahpach pashta | munach katon (gadol) ‖
5.	REVI'A	legarmeh | | munach revi'a ‖
6.	TEVIR	darga tevir (chefulah) ‖

*Connectors in the six groups above are: mercha, munach, mahpach, and darga.

**Separators in the six groups above are followed by one vertical line indicating 'pause' or two vertical lines indicating 'full stop'.

7. Additional connector neumes

ketanah   kadma   yerach-ben-yomo

8. Additional separator neumes

azla \| geireish \| gershayim \| pazeir \|

gedolah \| yetiv \| karnei-farah \| pesik \| \|
(silent)

EXAMPLE 3.4

Six groups of the 28 neumes, showing group-substitutes in parentheses, plus additional connectors* and separators**.

The other 21 neumes Rosowsky calls 'separators', meaning that the separator's motif and the following motif should be broken by a pause or full stop. This is shown in EXAMPLE 3.4,[14] where one vertical line (my insertion) indicates 'pause' and two vertical lines (again, my insertion) indicate 'full stop'. (The 28th neume, *pesik* |, meaning 'pause', has no sign other than the one vertical line, and is always silent).

Two of the connector-neumes—*mercha* and *munach*—assume a different musical garb depending on the separator-neume to which they connect. Some neume groups change motifs at the conclusion of Biblical books and chapters, and even during especially dramatic passages. The new motifs are generally triumphant-sounding or 'Jubilatory'.

In Appendix B, for instance, neume group 11. is used for chanting Exodus 15:1–21 (Song at the Sea) as well as Numbers 33:1–49 (Israel's wanderings in the wilderness). Both of these dramatic episodes are read to Jubilatory motifs.

Motif Variation

The main branches of world Jewry are: Ashkenazic (Northern European); Sephardic (Southern European); and Oriental (Non-Occidental). Among the many subdivisions of these branches are: German/Lithuanian (Ashkenazic, German being 'Western' and Lithuanian being 'Eastern'); Western Sephardic/Eastern Sephardic (Sephardic); and North African/Middle Eastern (Oriental). Each of these six subdivisions might have its own motif for each neume. The same is true for each off-shoot of the six subdivisions: English/Jerusalem (German/Lithuanian offshoots); Amsterdam/Balkan (Western/Eastern-Sephardic offshoots); Moroccan/Syrian (North African/Middle Eastern-Oriental offshoots).

Within most communities a different motif for each neume also exists for each of six different liturgical occasions. Torah has one set of motifs for weekday-Sabbath-Festival and another set for High Holy Day. The Torah portion of High Holy Day Festival, Sabbath, and fast days is followed by a Prophetic selection called Haftarah, related to it in content. Haftarah motifs differ from those of three "Scrolls" (*Megillot* in Hebrew), Ruth-Ecclesiastes-Song of Solomon, read during the three Pilgrimage Festivals. These differ in turn from either Lamentations, read on the fast of Tisha B'av (Ninth of Av), or Esther, read on the minor feast of Purim. The nomenclature for the different liturgical occasions (plus the Jubilatory fashion of reading) may be abbreviated as follows:

TOR	(Torah)
HHD	(High Holy Day)
FEST	(Festival
SAB	(Sabbath)
HAF	(Haftarah)
RES	(Ruth-Ecclesiates-Song of Solomon)
LAM	(Lamentations)
EST	(Esther)
JUB	(Jubilatory—for instance, a Jubilatory reading of Torah would be abbreviated JUB/TOR)

All the changes add up to 248 distinct motifs for every tradition. Multiply 248 by the main branches of world Jewry (Ashkenazic, Sephardic, Oriental), and by the limited subdivisions mentioned: (German/Lithuanian; Western Sephardic/Eastern Sephardic; North African/Middle Eastern). Multiply as well by subdivision offshoots such as English, Jerusalem, Amsterdam, Balkan, Moroccan, and Syrian, and the number of neume motifs is truly awesome.

Nomenclature for specific motif variants may be abbreviated by placing the first syllable of the divison or subdivision reading in superscript next to the liturgical occasion. Therefore, ^{Lith}TOR abbreviates Lithuanian Torah, ^{Ger}HAF abbreviates German Haftarah, and so forth. Appendix B limits itself to the Lithuanian tradition since most American congregations use one or another variant of it. Some vestigial overlapping of motifs exists among the diaspora traditions. This is to be expected, since we would like to believe that all motifs originated in the ancient Judean homeland. But overlapping is more than offset by the individual performance of each Bible reader, as he or she applies the motifs—memorized by means of neumes—to Scriptural passages sung differently at different times.

Of the six neume groups, the three most frequently heard are Sofpasuk, Etnachta, and Katon. A Bible verse cannot have more than one Sof-pasuk group (*sof-pasuk* means 'end-of-verse') nor more than one Etnachta group (*etnachta* signifies 'halfway rest'). But a verse may contain several Katon groups (*katon*, meaning 'small', indicates a slight upward melodic motion), as shown in EXAMPLE 3.5, a neume chart of Isaiah 40:3.

Note that the neume groups Sof-pasuk, Etnachta, and Katon, shown complete in Example 3.4, are truncated in Examples 3.5 and 3.6. In the first line of Examples 3.5 and 3.6, Katon group lacks its two opening neumes, *mahpach* and *pashta*`. In the second line, substitute separator *gadol* replaces the whole Katon group. Etnachta group (third line) and Katon group (fourth line) lack their respective opening neumes, *mercha* and *mahpach*. In the fifth line, Sof-pasuk group lacks its connector-neume, *mercha*, in two places: before *tipcha* and before *sof-pasuk* ⫶ . This often occurs in Scripture, depending on the text.

Number of group	Name of group	Name of neume	
4.	KATON	munach katon ‖	
4.	KATON	gadol (substitute separator) ‖	
2.	ETNACHTA	tipcha | munach etnachta ‖	
4.	KATON	pashta | munach katon ‖	
1.	SOF-PASUK	tipcha | sof-pasuk ‖	

EXAMPLE 3.5
Neume groups for chanting Isaiah 40:3.

EXAMPLE 3.6 gives Isaiah 40:3 in English translation, with the neumes indicated by signs above or below each word.

Number of group	Name of group	
4.	KATON	A-voice cries: ‖
4.	KATON	"In-the-wilderness (substitute separator) ‖
2.	ETNACHTA	prepare | the-way of-the-Lord;" ‖
4.	KATON	make-striaght | in the-desert ‖
1.	SOF-PASUK	a-highway | for-our-God." ‖

EXAMPLE 3.6
Isaiah 40:3, in English, with neumes.

Now compare two Ashkenazic readings of the same Haftarah verse, the Lithuanian tradition after Rosowsky (EXAMPLE 3.7a);[15] and the German tradition transcribed by Idelsohn (EXAMPLE 3.7b.)[16] The sequence of neume groups is the same for all traditions, hence the phrasing remains identical. However, different motifs are shown for the neumes in each example. From Example 3.7 we can see that most of the motifs for each neume are quite different, due to the influence of their respective host cultures. Lithuanian folk song (along with that of Poland and Russia) generally uses minor modes,[17] while German folk song generally uses major modes. The text is the first half of Isaiah 40:3 in its original Hebrew:

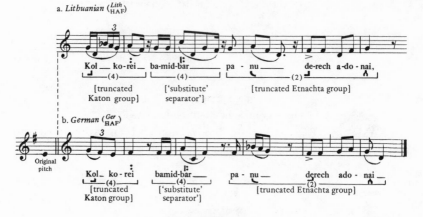

EXAMPLE 3.7
Comparing Lithuanian and German neume motifs
for the first half of Isaiah 40:3.

Interchangeability of Psalmodic and Biblical Techniques

Psalmodic technique sometimes spills over into Scripture reading, just as Biblical technique often crops up in prayer. For instance, a Torah reader can "improvise" the assigned portion by declaiming the bulk of every verse on Psalmodic reciting-tones, quoting an occasional separator-neume motif to give the reading authentic flavor. And the reader can get through the passage in one-half to one-third the time if the situation merits it.

Likely candidates for this approach are the many lengthy passages dealing with sacrificial rites. Leviticus 4:3 is typical:

> *Im hakohein hamashi'ach yecheta . . .*
> 'If it is the anointed priest who sins, thus
> bringing guilt on the people, then let him
> offer for the sin which he has committed a
> young bull without blemish to the Lord for a
> sin offering'.

EXAMPLE 3.8a uses standard Biblical technique with the verse, after [Lith]TOR.[18] If we sing it *mf*, at an *Andante*, or 'walking' tempo, approximately 33 seconds will elapse from beginning to end.

EXAMPLE 3.8b uses Psalmodic technique with the same verse, choosing vocally comfortable reciting-tones ($\underline{A}$ and $\underline{G}$) for each half-

EXAMPLE 3.8
Torah reading prepared as Biblical chant,
and "improvised" as Psalmodic chant.

verse. In place of the customary halfway-rest neume, *etnachta*, Example 3.8b enlists *gädol*; in place of the customary verse-ending neume, *sof-pasuk*, it enlists *revi'a*. Both substitutions are picked to retain the expected sound of [Lith]TOR; other separator-neume motifs would probably work as well. When this "improvised" version of Leviticus 4:3 is sung *mp*, at an *Allegro*, or fast (literally 'cheerful') tempo, it takes about 11 seconds, one-third the time of Biblical Example 3.8a.

If Psalmodic technique may enter Bible reading through the use of reciting-tones, so too Biblical technique enters prayer through the use of neume motifs. The Night-prayer, *Hashkiveinu* ('Cause us, O God, to lie down in peace'), which appears in many Maariv services sung in American synagogues, is a case in point.

EXAMPLE 3.9a[19] represents numerous *Hashkiveinu* settings penned by the coloratura-bass cantor and teacher, Adolpho Katchko, who died in New York City in 1958. Our illustration begins with the second verse of *Hashkiveinu*. Each half-verse follows the classic Psalmodic pattern: brief initial figure; reciting-tone; melodic flourish.

> *Uferos aleinu sukkat shelomecha . . .*
> 'Spread over us thy tabernacle of peace,
> direct us aright through thy good counsel'.

EXAMPLE 3.9b[20] is by the 19th-century cantor of Odessa, Jacob Bachmann (1846–1905), who possessed a wide-ranging heroic tenor. Bachmann uses the neumatic (Biblical) technique of note-grouping as well as specific neume motifs in rendering *Hashkiveinu*. Instead of dividing each verse into two balanced halves, he strings five neume-like motifs over the full verse-length, indicating it is to be sung *Andante*, *mf*, exactly the pace and dynamic of Biblical chant, as we have seen.

EXAMPLE 3.9c[21] shows how it is possible to identify every phrase in Example 3.9b as modified [Ger]HAF neume motifs.

Misinai Tunes: Evolution

Insertion of neume motifs into Prayer chant is an established feature of synagogue practice everywhere. Between the years 1095 and 1272, Jewish Rhineland communities bordering Southwestern Germany and Northeastern France were devastated by Christian Crusaders. The cantors of those communities composed prayers that expressed both their despair and God's glory. Litanies begging forgiveness from sin (else why

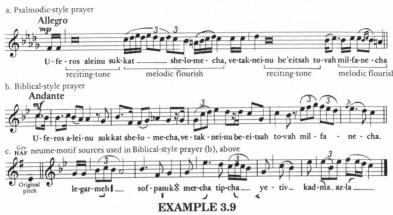

EXAMPLE 3.9

Prayer, chanted Psalmodically (using reciting-tones and melodic flourishes), and Biblically (using modified German-Haftarah neume motifs).

was God punishing them?) were called *selichot*, from the Hebrew *selichah* ('forgiveness'). Paeans to the Almighty—whose power alone could deliver from imminent doom—were called *piyyutim* (from Piyyut, 'poetry', evidently derived from the Greek *poites*, 'poet'). Both *selichot* and *piyyutim* had existed for hundreds of years, first in Palestine, later in Babylonia, Spain, and Italy. But those written by eyewitnesses to the crusaders' atrocities used the oldest melorhythmic fragments known to their composers: Biblical neume motifs.

Jewish tradition categorizes most ancient practices under the heading, *Misinai* (literally 'from Mount Sinai'), as if God had handed them down to Moses with the other commandments in the Torah. Since Bible-reading in the German-speaking communities was already ancient at the time of the Crusades, its neume motifs were considered *Misinai*. Even today this group of prayer motifs is called *Nigunei Misinai*, or 'Tunes from Mount Sinai'.

By the middle of the 14th century, at the time of the Black Death that swept through Europe, over 200 Rhineland communities had fled to the Eastern European countries of Poland, Russia, and the Balkans. The poetic texts of the *Misinai* Tunes, commemorating Rhineland martyrdoms, had no relevance in those countries, and were discarded. But their melodies—neume motifs of the German Scripture-reading tradition—seemed strangely familiar, and immediately entered the great body of *Keva* prayers recited by all Jews since the days of the Second Temple. Why did the Rhineland neume motifs sound familiar? What follows is an educated guess.

Eastern European Jews stemmed originally (circa first century) from the Caucasus, later (circa sixth century) from the Byzantine provinces.[22] Their countries of origin all follow Middle Eastern practice, whose singing features microtonal inflections and ornamentation, rather than long-held notes.[23] This tonally-dense approach continued to infuse both their Scripture reading and Prayer chant long after the settlers had spread northward and westward to the Balkans, Russia, and Poland.

At the same time, Western European Jews in the Rhineland were following the Tiberian system of Biblical *te'amim*, and deferring to rabbinical authorities in Palestine,[24] their land of origin. Scripture reading influenced Prayer chant, as did the surrounding folk music, which reflected Occidental emphasis of harmonic—as opposed to melodic—considerations. Each successive interval in a melody might also outline a chord, and so imply changing harmonies.[25] As a result, individual notes are generally sustained, imparting a sparser tonal density to the singing.

When Rhineland Jews migrated eastward, beginning in the 12th century, their *Misinai* Tunes—the only element of their sacred chant to have escaped what Idelsohn calls 'Germanization'—were adopted as Prayer motifs by their Eastern European brethren. The latter, however, "retained the decidedly Oriental strain of their music"[26] in their Scripture reading.

No written evidence of Middle Eastern Scripture reading has survived from the 14th century. Nevertheless, change does not occur quickly in that culture sphere, especially in the reading of Scripture, a community's most zealously guarded heritage. Thus we may regard even contemporary Middle Eastern Torah reading as indicative of a particular style formed centuries earlier. Middle Eastern singing style is free and ornate, maintaining interest through an ever-changing succession of rapidly-delivered and closely-spaced tones. EXAMPLE 3.10a[27] records a 20th-century Turkish-Jewish reading of Leviticus 16:1–2 ([Turk]TOR), probably similar to the Biblical chant brought north from the Caucasus and Byzantine provinces, and practiced by Jewish communities in the Slavic lands during the Middle Ages.

1. Vaidabeir adonai el-mosheh . . .

'The Lord spoke to Moses after the death
of the two sons of Aaron . . .' .

2. *Vayomer adonai . . .*
'And the Lord said . . .'.

Observe the high degree of ornamentation, 59 notes in four melismas (bold): *vaida**beir** el-moshèh*; *acharei **mòt***; and *ado**nai*** , for an average tone density of almost 15 notes on each of those ornamented syllables (bracketed: Compare to the average tone density of [Lith]HAF in Example 3.2b, a mere four notes per word).

We do have an early 16th-century notation of [Ger]TOR no doubt similar to that practiced by German-speaking Rhineland communities between the 12th and 14th centuries (EXAMPLE 3.10b).[28] In conformity with Western European singing style, it is regular and unadorned. Note the successive bracketed intervals of thirds: D–F initially (*Vaida**beir***), followed by F–A (*ado-**nai***), reversed A–F (*el-**moshèh***), and repeated A–F (*acharei-**mòt***). The intervals of thirds succeed one another in a steady, prolonged intonation, creating a semi-chordal effect. The congregation participates by humming words in an undertone on F throughout the

EXAMPLE 3.10
Torah reading in two traditions; Turkish ([Turk]TOR); and German ([Ger]TOR).

reading. (See **PART I, JERUSALEM OF OLD:** *The Congregational 'Drone'*). The ^{Ger}TOR tone density of Example 3.10b, only two notes each for the same four syllables that were ornamented in Example 3.10a, is even less than the ^{Lith}HAF tone density of Example 3.2b, which was four notes per syllable. Lower tone density implies slower tempo and fuller sound.

Yet for all the surface differences between the 20th-century ^{Turk}TOR and its 16th-century ^{Ger}TOR counterpart, likenesses among the neume motifs emerge once we strip away the ornamental notes.

In both, the outline of *munach katon* (*acharei mot*, fourth measure) is: G–A–F. Too, the melodic curves of *tipcha* (*mishenei*, fifth measure) are almost identical: D–F–D compared to F–F–D, as is the contour of *munach etnachta* (*benei aharon*, fourth measure), essentially: D–G–F in both. Only at the mention of God's name (*adonai*, final word) does ^{Turk}TOR diverge, brandishing 31 notes compared to seven, a license not permitted in the Western European style of ^{Ger}TOR.

On reflection, it really should come as no surprise that the Eastern Ashkenazic Jews appropriated *Misinai* Tunes for prayer and ornate singing during Scripture reading; both elements conceivably descended from ancient Judean secular usage. The heritage had come full circle: Middle Eastern-in-Rhineland Biblical chant; to Middle Eastern-Eastern European Prayer chant. Ever since the 14th century, *Misinai* Tunes have been used by both subdivisions of Ashkenazic Jewry in prayer. We deal with Prayer modes primarily in **PART III** of this book (**MODAL TECHNIQUE**). But because *Misinai* Tunes so closely parallel neume motifs, we introduce them here.

EXAMPLE 3.11 shows 18 Prayer-types sung to *Misinai* Tunes in America today, grouped by category and section of their occurrence. **I. STATUTORY PRAYERS** (*Tefillot Keva*), formulated between –500 and –200, are oldest.[29] **II. LAUDATORY POEMS** (*Piyyutim*), which first appeared in the fifth century, come next. **III. PENITENTIAL LAMENTS** (*Selichot*), many of which stem from Scripture, were introduced with Statutory prayers, but because of continuing persecutions (in Nazi Germany), are still being written. Reform and Conservative American Jews omit most of the Hebrew *Piyyutim* and *Selichot* in their services; Orthodox Jews retain most of both categories in their original Hebrew. But whenever a congregation from any of the three movements sings *Misinai* material, the mood is palpably different.

PRAYER-TYPE	SERVICE(S) OF PRIMARY OCCURRENCE

I. STATUTORY PRAYERS	*(Tefillot Keva)*	
-a- 'Call to Prayer'	*(Barechu)*	HHD and FEST Maariv
-b- 'Credo'	*(Shema)*	HHD Maariv, Torah, and Neilah
-c- 'Patriarchal Prayer'	*(Avot)*	HHD Shacharit, Musaf, and Minchah
-d- 'Sanctification'	*(Kedushah)*	HHD Shacharit, Musaf, Minchah, and Neilah
-e- 'Adoration'	*(Aleinu)*	HHD Musaf Amidah ('Standing Devotion')
-f- 'Doxology'	*(Kaddish)*	HHD Torah and Musaf

II. LAUDATORY POEMS	*(Piyyutim)*	
-g- 'Concerning "The Creator of Light" '	*(Me'orah)*	HHD, FEST, and SAB Shacharit
-h- 'Concerning "Angels" '	*(Ofan)*	HHD, FEST, and SAB Shacharit
-i- 'Concerning "Redemption" '	*(Zulat/Ge'ulah)*	HHD, FEST, and SAB Shacharit
-j- 'Concerning "Divine Permission" '	*(Reshut)*	
-k- 'Concerning "Shield of Abraham" '	*(Magein)*	
-l- 'Concerning "Resurrection" '	*(Mechayeh)*	HHD, FEST, and SAB Shacharit and Musaf
-m- 'Concerning "Tripartite Sanctification" '		(plus Minchah and Neilah on Yom Kippur)
	(Meshulash)	
-n- 'Concerning "Heavenly Ascent" '	*(Siluk)*	

III. PENITENTIAL LAMENTS	*(Selichot)*	
-o- 'Individual Biblical verse'	*(Pasuk)*	Minor fasts: Shacharit and Minchah;
-p- 'Grouped Biblical verses'	*(Sidrei Pesukim)*	Month of Elul: pre-dawn; Yom Kippur:
-q- 'Individual composed verse'	*(Selichah)*	Maariv, Shacharit, Musaf, Minchah, and
-r- 'Grouped composed verses'	*(Sidrei Selichot)*	Neilah

EXAMPLE 3.11

Eighteen Prayer-types sung to *Misinai* Tunes, and service(s) where sung.

Misinai Tunes: Variations

The 39 *Misinai* Tunes (as I have catalogued them in Appendix C; others may list more or less), like their parent neume motifs, stand suspended between the worlds of theory and practice; they are musical themes subject to endless variations. Every cantor articulates their intervals, rhythm, and dynamic differently, just as every Scripture reader applies the neume motifs differently to a given text. Worshippers, conditioned to expect individual interpretation at specific moments in prayer, respond as to nothing else—such is the power of the *Misinai* element in Ashkenazic Synagogue song.

Israeli scholar Hanoch Avenary underscores the challenge which *Misinai* Tunes pose for every cantor: to improvise creatively on a musical idea.

There is no 'archetype' for any of the *Misinai Nigunim*; only different 'realizations' of a certain image.[30]

Performance method is more "Oriental" than "Occidental." So is the plasticity of rhythm exhibited by both *Misinai* and Biblical motifs. In Occidental music, one motif is often repeated with variations. In Oriental music, motifs are generally strung together, each with its own rhythmic pattern. Thus to transcribe Prayer chant with its *Misinai* Tunes, or Scripture reading with its neume motifs—in conventional Western fashion—requires encapsulating each motif in its own measure, with its own meter, dynamic, and tempo. The procedure is inefficient compared to using neumes (*te'amim*) to indicate Biblical motifs, and Prayer-type nomenclature (with or without the numeration in Appendix C, which is my own) to indicate *Misinai* Tunes.

As an illustration of how *Misinai* Tunes can vary, consider the Yom Kippur Eve prayer, Kol Nidre ('All Vows'), which Abraham Idelsohn calls the most characteristic of all Synagogue tunes.[31] Kol Nidre happens to be a Penitential Lament (see Category III., Prayer-type –r–, in Example 3.11 and Appendix C), a series of composed rather than Scriptural verses asking *selichah* (forgiveness) for not fulfilling personal vows to God. A glance at Appendix C demonstrates that Kol Nidre includes seven Primary Occurrences of *Misinai* Tunes.

This richness of *Misinai* Tunes far exceeds any other text, and would seem to indicate a fairly fixed form. Yet no two identical versions of Kol Nidre to my knowledge have ever been published. Neither the shape assumed by its 13 *Misinai* Tunes, nor the sequence of their appearance, is duplicated in the hundreds of settings performed by cantors all over the world.

Look at the key phrase in Kol Nidre, asking forgiveness. In four of the oldest published versions of the text, note how markedly this one phrase differs.

> *miyom kippurim zeh ...*
> 'from this Day of Atonement until
> the coming one'.

EXAMPLE 3.12a,[32] from 1791, uses a version of *Misinai* Tune 15;
EXAMPLE 3.12b,[33] from 1839, uses a version of *Misinai* Tune 39;
EXAMPLE 3.12c,[34] from 1847, uses versions of *Misinai* Tunes 5 and 27;
EXAMPLE 3.12d,[35] from 1877, uses versions of *Misinai* Tunes 39 and 37.

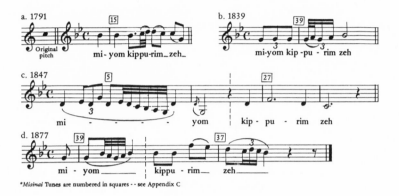

Misinai Tunes are numbered in squares - - see Appendix C

EXAMPLE 3.12
A single phrase from four of the oldest published Kol Nidre settings,
using five different *Misinai* Tunes.

Misinai Tunes: Occurrences

Misinai Tunes help Ashkenazic Jews approach God in two ways,
through prayers of praise and through prayers of petition. In Example
3.11, the first two categories—Statutory Prayers and Laudatory
Poems—list prayers of praise; the third category—Penitential Laments—lists prayers of petition. All may enlist *Misinai* Tunes to em-
phasize God's might and/or man's weakness. All recur throughout the
year's liturgy, chanted on different occasions, according to prescribed
Prayer modes (see **PART III**).

EXAMPLE 3.13a[36] cites the Primary Occurrence of *Misinai* Tune
3 within Rosh Hashanah Maariv (see Appendix C, left-hand column).
The text of Example 3.13a concludes the first paragraph following
Barechu, or 'Call to Prayer', and is thus considered a *Barechu*-type.

> *Uma'avir yom umeivi lailah*
> 'Thou makest the day pass and night to
> approach'.

EXAMPLE 3.13b[37] offers a Recurrence of *Misinai* Tune 3 (see Appendix C, center column, third Recurrence), this time in Psalm 67:5,
sung as a Sabbath-night Piyyut prior to Maariv.

Yoducha amim . . .
'Let all the people praise thee, O God, let all
peoples praise thee'.

EXAMPLE 3.13c[34] shows *Misinai* Tune ⃞3 used in a *Selichah*, during
Neilah, the concluding Yom Kippur service (see Appendix C, center
column, fourth Recurrence). The text which it accompanies is from Exodus 34:6 and 34:9. Contrite man, having fasted for more than 24 hours,
petitions God one last time to forgive his sins.

Adonai, adonai . . .
6. 'The Lord, the Lord,
a God merciful and gracious . . .
9. pardon our iniquity'.

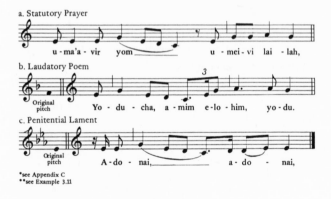

a. Statutory Prayer

u - ma'a - vir   yom____   u - mei - vi lai - lah,

b. Laudatory Poem

Original pitch   Yo - du - cha, a - mim e -lo - him,   yo - du.

c. Penitential Lament

Original pitch   A - do - nai,____   a - do - nai,

*see Appendix C
**see Example 3.11

EXAMPLE 3.13
Misinai Tune ⃞3 * as it occurs in all three Prayer categories.**

Solemn in intent, the *Misinai* Tunes are wonderful to sing wherever
they occur, stirring even a casual synagogue-goer into the proper mood.
As demonstrated in Example 3.13, a single *Misinai* Tune ⃞3 can portray:
God's control of nature (3.13a); God's power over mankind (3.13b); as
well as man's sincere repentance (3.13c). The next chapter shows how
another Misinai Tune (⃞21) appears in four diverse parts of the liturgy.

Tone Density; Neumes; *Misinai* Tunes: Bibliography & Notes

1. SIFRA: (Midrash on Leviticus 23:44) "And Moses declared the set feasts of the Lord unto the Children of Israel." ACTS: (15:21) "From early generations Moses had in every city those who preach him, for he is read every Sabbath in the Synagogue." For fuller documentation see Hyman I. SKY: *The Development of the Office of Hazzan through the Talmudic Period*, Philadelphia, Dropsie University (1977), pages 23–24.

2. BAYER, Bathya: "Cantillation," *Encyclopedia Judaica*, Jerusalem, Keter (1972), Volume 5:127–129.

3. SACHS, Curt: *The Rise of Music in the Ancient World, East and West*, New York, Norton (1943), page 83; first came line patterns, then word-motifs. That Psalmodic Chant antedates Biblical Chant may be inferred from the fact that it dominates Bukharan TOR (see IDELSOHN: *Thesaurus*, III: number 138), and Yemenite EST (see IDELSOHN, *Thesaurus*, I: number 126), both traditions being preserved relatively intact since ancient times.

4. SULZER, Salomon: *Schir Zion* (Vienna, 1839–1865), revised by Joseph Sulzer, Vienna, (1905), number 26.

5. ALTER, Israel: *The Sabbath Service*, New York, Cantors Assembly (1968), page 12.

6. FRIEDMANN, Aron: *Schir Lisch'laumau*, Berlin, Deutsche-Israelitischen Gemeindebunde (1901), number 139.

7. KATZ, Sholom: *Haben Yakir Li*, recording, New York, Kellet KLP–1511, side A, band 4; transcribed by Joseph A. Levine.

8. ROSOWSKY, Solomon: *Neume Motifs for the Yearly Cycle of Biblical Chant, According to the Lithuanian Tradition*, after manuscripts, New York, Jewish Theological Seminary (1958); Appendix B, line II HAF, motifs 7.c, 7.d, 8.a, 5.c.

9. APEL, Willi: "Trope," *Harvard Dictionary of Music*, Second Edition, 1972:871.

10. NEUMES: After *Webster's Third New Dictionary*, 1981:1520; and *Harvard Dictionary of Music*, 1972:571.

11. MALAVSKY, Samuel: *Veshameru*, recording, New York, Banner BAS–1012, side A, band 2; transcribed by Joseph A. Levine.

12. ROSOWSKY (see item 8), line II HAF, motif groups 6. and 1.

13. MARGOLIS, Max L.: "Accents in Hebrew," *Jewish Encyclopedia*, New York, Funk & Wagnalls (1901), Volume I:156.

14. ROSOWSKY, Solomon: *The Cantillation of the Bible*, New York, Reconstructionist (1957), pages 606–613.

15. ROSOWSKY (see item 8), line II HAF, motifs 4.:c,d,e; 2.:c,d.

16. IDELSOHN, Abraham Zvi: *Jewish Music*, New York, Holt (1929), page 53, Example 5.

17. NETTL, Bruno: *Folk and Traditional Music of the Western Contintents*, Englewood Cliffs, Prentice-Hall, Second Edition (1973), page 99.

18. ROSOWSKY (see item 8), line I throughout.

54 • SYNAGOGUE SONG IN AMERICA

** •   SYNAGOGUE SONG IN AMERICA**

19. KATCHKO, Adolph: *Hashkiveinu*, manuscript, New York, Hebrew Union College (circa 1950).
20. BACHMANN, Jacob: *Schirath Jacob*, Odessa, Jurgenson (1884), number 17.
21. COHEN, Francis Lyon: "Cantillation," *Jewish Encyclopedia*, New York, Funk & Wagnalls (1903), Volume III:540; 545; 541; 544. IDELSOHN, Abraham Zvi: *Toledot Haneginah Ha'ivrit*, Tel Aviv, Dvir (1924), page 193, line 9.
22. IDELSOHN (see item 16), page 182; DUBNOW, Simon M.: *History of the Jews in Russia and Poland*, translated from the Russian by Israel Friedlaender, Philadelphia, Jewish Publication Society (1916), page 18.
23. IDELSOHN (see item 16), page 25; AVENARY, Hanoch: *Studies in the Hebrew, Syrian, and Greek Liturgical Recitative*, Tel Aviv, Israel Music Institute (1963), page 21.
24. AVENARY (see item 23), page 30.
25. *GROVE'S Dictionary Of Music And Musicians:* edited by Eric Blom, New York, St. Martins, Fifth Edition (1966), page 667.
26. IDELSOHN (see item 16), page 183.
27. KOLINSKI, M.: "Notes on Music," *Folk Music of Palestine*, recording, New York, Ethnic Folkways P408, side 1, band 8.
28. BOESCHENSTEIN, Johannes: Transcription of [Ger]TOR neume motifs, in Johannes Reuchlin's *De Accentibus et Orthographia Linguae Hebraicae*, Hagenau (1518); charted by Hanoch AVENARY, in *The Ashkenazi Tradition of Biblical Chant Between 1500 and 1900*, Tel Aviv, Ministry of Education (1978), line 1, throughout. Avenary's study points to continuity in [Ger]TOR motifs since the late-10th century, when the Tiberian system of 28 *te'amim* was first adopted by Western Ashkenazic Jewry.
29. SPERBER, Daniel: "The Great Synagogue," *Encyclopedia Judaica*, Jerusalem, Keter (1972), Volume 15:629–630.
30. AVENARY, Hanoch: "Mis-Sinai Nigginum," *Encyclopedia Judaica*, Jerusalem, Keter (1972), Volume 12:153.
31. IDELSOHN, Abraham: "The Kol Nidre Tune," *Hebrew Union College Annual*, Cincinnati (1931-1932), Volumes 8–9, pages 493–509.
32. BEER, Aaron: (Berlin, 1791), published in Idelsohn (see item 31), Example 1.
33. SULZER (see item 4), number 111.
34. NAUMBOURG, Samuel: *Chants religieux des Israëlites*, Paris, published by the author (1847), number 4.
35. BAER, Abraham: *Baal T'fillah*, Gothenburg, published by the author (1877), number 1301.
36. BIRNBAUM, Abraham Ber: *Amanut Hachazanut*, Czestochowa, published by the author (1912), number 2.
37. SULZER (see item 4), number 153.
38. SULZER (see item 4), number 457.

CHAPTER FOUR

The Many Faces of Neume Motifs

The motifs and methods of Scripture reading have had a significant influence on Jewish culture in Europe and in the United States. In this chapter we continue to explore how the singing of Biblical figurations varies by region, occasion, and type of voice. After tracking two linked motifs, we provide examples of others in folk song, theater and a wedding march.

An Adaptable Approach

Well-prepared Bible chant reflects a thousand years of students reading aloud and chanting to each other in the study halls of European synagogues.[1] In Lithuania as late as 1800, the musical reading of Scripture to prescribed patterns of neumes was a Jewish child's first formal exposure to music-making. Neume motifs straddle the line bordering written and oral tradition. In printed editions of the Bible, they indicate note groupings more-or-less fixed by convention. In the mouth of a genuinely musical reader, however, Bible chant can not only vary but also be a deeply moving experience.

Five Regional Traditions

As Jewish immigrants from all over the world settled in America, bringing with them their separate Scripture-reading practices, cantors here had a cornucopia of sounds and styles from which to choose. As evidence of the options possible for even one verse of Torah, we will look at five regional approaches for chanting Genesis 39:5: the German, English, Baltimore, Lithuanian, and Jerusalem traditions.

*Vaiȟi mai'az*ᵃ *hifkid oťo beveiťo* . . .

'From the time that he made him overseer in
his house and over all that he had, the Lord
blessed the Egyptian's house for Joseph's
sake; the blessing of the Lord was upon all
that he had, in house and field'.

EXAMPLE 4.1a[2] demonstrates the German tradition (ᴳᵉʳTOR), EXAMPLE 4.1b[3] the English tradition (ᴱⁿᵍTOR, an alternate version of the German). EXAMPLE 4.1c[4] shows the Baltimore tradition (ᴮᵃˡᵗTOR). EXAMPLE 4.1d[5] gives the Lithuanian tradition, (thoroughly documented in Appendix B), and EXAMPLE 4.1e[6] shows the Jerusalem tradition (ᴶᵉʳTOR), an alternate version of the Lithuanian. The conventional notation indicates only relative time division, as in Gregorian chant—each phrase may be sung *A piacere* ('As you please')—in step with the Biblical argument. Rather than mark off metrical units, the double-bar lines (I I) separate motifs—21 in Example 4.1—for easier identification. Each motif has been assigned a circled number for discussion later. The neumes themselves are written above or below the transliterated Hebrew text.

The Baltimore tradition (Example 4.1c) highlights traits of the other traditions as well. It achieves a compromise by tempering the longer note-values and larger intervals of the two Western European traditions (ᴳᵉʳTOR and ᴱⁿᵍTOR) with the wider range and more impetuous rhythm of the two Eastern European traditions (ᴸⁱᵗʰTOR and ᴶᵉʳTOR).

Its *munach etnachta* pause (neume motifs ⑬ and ⑭), has the ᴳᵉʳTOR and ᴱⁿᵍTOR sound of a minor mode, moving up tranquilly from D in motif ⑬ to F in motif ⑭ . Its *sof-pasuk* ⫶ stop (motif ㉑) is a tonic-major ending on F, as in all other traditions except ᴸⁱᵗʰTOR (which drops to C).

We have already observed this basic East/West dichotomy at work in Lithuanian and German traditions (see Example 3.7). Baltimore's

Etnachta-group Separator *tipcha* (motif ⑳), effects a similar recon-
ciliation, this time between ^{Ger}TOR rhythm and ^{Jer}TOR melody.

Chronology of the Five Traditions

In Example 4.1, the neume combination of *kadma azlá* (motifs ③ and
④) illustrates nicely the chronological progression from small-to-large
intervals and narrow-to-wide range. ^{Ger}TOR *kadma azlá* follows
musicologist Joseph Yasser's description of early chant: mostly one note
per syllable (syllabic); motion up or down one step at a time (diatonic);
its range confined to the interval of a fifth (pentachord) or less.[7] ^{Eng}TOR
kadma azlá expands this range to an octave. At first glance the narrow
range of ^{Balt}TOR and ^{Lith}TOR *kadma azlá*, only a sixth (F–D), would
seem to place them chronologically between ^{Ger}TOR and ^{Eng}TOR. But
the prominence of their ascending major triad, F–A–C (with ^{Lith}TOR ar-
riving at C via an accented grace-note, or *appoggiatura*, on D), dates
them late. ^{Jer}TOR is latest of all, leaping an open fifth, F–C, on *kadma*.

Medium (baritone/mezzo) and High (tenor/soprano) Voices

The German tradition of Torah reading (Example 4.1) lies completely
within a medium voice's most resonant range, middle C to D a ninth
above. Since the duties of German cantors historically included Torah
reading, and the preferences of German-speaking congregations for
decorum precluded ornamental singing (in which higher-voiced cantors
are wont to indulge),[8] it is easy to see why baritone cantors were the
norm in Western Europe. ^{Ger}TOR and ^{Eng}TOR in fact present no
problems to medium-voiced singers (most of us). Another reason why
German-speaking congregations sought baritone cantors was the
phenomenal success of Salomon Sulzer, whose active years in Vienna
stretched over half a century, 1826–1881. Eric Werner classifies Sulzer's
voice as a "high baritone of mellow quality, typical of the German
oratorio."[9]

The lyric tenor voice offered a different ideal of cantorial sonority. Better suited to ^{Lith}TOR and ^{Jer}TOR, it was exemplified by Sulzer's contemporary, Nisi Blumenthal, who served as cantor in Odessa from 1840
to 1892. To understand the reasons for this different ideal, study the
neume combination *munach katon* (motifs ⑱ and ⑲ , and the Sep-
arator *tipcha* (motif ⑳), of Example 4.1. In ^{Ger}TOR, ^{Eng}TOR, and
^{Balt}TOR, upward motion does not exceed A,—in ^{Lith}TOR and ^{Jer}TOR, it

EXAMPLE 4.1
Five Traditions of Ashkenazic Torah reading ([Ash]TOR).

EXAMPLE 4.1, *continued.*

reaches C twice. Downward motion in ^{Ger}TOR, ^{Eng}TOR, and ^{Balt}TOR is stepwise: A–G; G–F; or at most, by thirds: A–F; F–D. ^{Lith}TOR and ^{Jer}TOR twice skip downward in fourths within just three sequential motifs, ⑱ – ⑳ .

That skip of a fourth, up or down (G–C or C–G), happens to coincide with the medium voice's most open sounds (called *vuoto*, or 'empty' in Italian, because of their effortless production).[10] In the previous chapter we discussed the frequency with which the neumes *munach katòn* and *tipcha* occur, about twice as often as other neumes (see Example 3.5). In Example 4.1 they figure eight times out of 21, or 38 percent, including *pashtà*, the Separator which always precedes *katòn*.

Baritones and mezzos might do well to avoid both ^{Lith}TOR and ^{Jer}TOR, lest they find themselves booming forth Scripture in the loudest part of their voice over a third of the time, an effect wearing on both reader and listeners. Tenors and sopranos, on the other hand, need not worry about the leaping intervals G–C or C–G which lie congenially in their voice. The various traditions suit voices differently; ^{Balt}TOR, in this writer's opinion, best suits the baritone/mezzo majority while maintaining the solemnity so essential to Scripture reading.

Prayer moves similarly upward in vocal register the further east its provenance. The key phrase of Musaf Kedushah will demonstrate:

> *Vehu yashmi'einu . . .*
> 'And He in his mercy will again
> proclaim to us:
> "I am your God" '.

EXAMPLE 4.2 shows the five traditions of Example 4.1, this time in prayer, running the gamut from low-and-deliberate to high-and-rapid. EXAMPLE 4.2a,[11] by Louis Lewandowsky of Berlin, is obviously intended for low baritone (women did not begin to function as cantors until a century after this piece was written in 1871). EXAMPLE 4.2b,[12] by Samuel Alman of London, will suit any medium voice. EXAMPLE 4.2c,[13] by Abba Weisgal of Baltimore, covers the same ground as Example 4.2b, but moves stepwise. (Formerly of Ivancice, Czechoslovakia, and trained in Vienna, Weisgal became one of the foremost modern spokespersons for the high-baritone tradition in Bible chant [Baltimore] as well as in prayer [Sulzer]). EXAMPLE 4.2d,[14] by Yehoshua Ne'eman of Jerusalem, extends the stepwise motion upward to a full octave, for tenor. EXAMPLE 4.2e,[15] by Moshe Koussevitsky of Smorgon in

Lithuania, carries rapid Eastern European-style singing to its highest pinnacle; his was considered by many to be the most extraordinary cantorial tenor of recent times (1899–1966). In this example, two of the Ashkenazic regions (Lithuania and Jerusalem) are reversed: Ashkenazic prayer-tradition 4. is Jerusalemic, and Prayer-tradition 5. is Lithuanian, to better illustrate the progression upward in pitch.

EXAMPLE 4.2
Five traditions of Ashkenazic prayer.

During the 19th century, Salomon Sulzer's high-baritone chazanic style spread west of Vienna, but it never took root in the east. Cantors in the Slavic countries were almost all tenors, as seen in Examples 4.2d and 4.2e; the music written by them or for them requires a high, flexible voice. The two million Eastern European Jews who emigrated to the United States between 1880 and 1924 continued to demand a tenor cantor, because the sound reminded them of their old tradition.

In the last 100 years, practically all world-class cantors who flourished in America have been tenors. However, they have often refused to do Bible chant, leaving Scripture reading to the sexton (*shamash*) or to laymen, saving themselves for prayer, especially during the late-morning Musaf when attendance is greater. The Lithuanian tradition of Bible chant, preserved so assiduously in America by Solomon Rosowsky, is taught at cantorial seminaries, but it survives more in theory than in practice, for most students have baritone or mezzo voices and cannot execute it properly. The Jerusalem variant of Lithuanian tradition persists in Israel, where cantors and worshippers of Eastern European extraction delight in the high-pitched sounds still fresh in their memory.

Dramatizing Bible Chant

Skilled readers use many devices to dramatize the chanting of Biblical passages. Typical are two verses from the *Megillah* of Esther, recounting Israel's deliverance from royally-decreed genocide in ancient Persia. EST is read on the late-winter festival of Purim—which always falls on a weekday—when it is permissible to indulge in merrymaking. Hence the reader's delivery covers a wide dramatic spectrum: from singsong to declamation; from whispered *pianissimo* to thundering *fortissimo*.

EXAMPLE 4.3 transcribes the reading of Cantor Abba Weisgal of Baltimore. Sung at an actual Purim Eve service, this Example illustrates a frequently-used dramatic style.[16] Drawn from the second half of Esther 5:9, it reads as follows:

$$vechir'ot^Q \quad ha\grave{m}an \; et\text{-}mordech\acute{a}i \ldots$$

'but when Haman saw Mor'decai in the
King's gate, that he neither rose nor
trembled before him, he was filled with
wrath against Mor'decai'.

For the passage in brackets in Example 4.3a, where **x**-signs replace the notes, the reader growls rather than sings Haman's wrath against Mor'decai. The **x**-signs indicate speech as much as song; the technique is called *Sprechgesang* ('speech-song') in German. EXAMPLE 4.3b shows neume motifs for the 4.3a-passage in brackets, should readers prefer using traditional EST chant throughout. Weisgal's EST chant is close to the prevalent American tradition, [Lith]EST (pitched a note higher, on E, in Appendix B, line VI EST). Verse 7:3 of Esther reads as follows:

Im-matsati chein be'einecha
hamělech . . .

'[Then Queen Esther answered,] "If I have
found favor in your sight, O King, and if it
please the King, let my life be given me at my
petition, and my people at my request" '.

In EXAMPLE 4.3c the reader uses a despairing tone, to intensify Queen
Esther's plea. This is achieved by changing both the voice and the musical mode. The voice changes from "singing" to "speaking" by dropping
motif-endings at *Im-matsati . . .* ('If-I-have-found-favor') and again at
hamělech ('the King'), both instances marked by double-slur lines ( )))
downward to an indefinite pitch. The musical mode changes from

EXAMPLE 4.3
Dramatized readings from Esther (EST).

"bright" E♭ major to "dark" E♭ minor, at the passage in brackets, beginning with *tináten* ('let-my-life-be-given-me'), and the mood changes from light-hearted banter to life-and-death pleading. In effect, a lament has replaced EST chant through one chromatically-altered note: B♮ instead of B♭ at the end of *bish'eilaii* ('at-my-petition'). (The lament-like E♭-minor mode, known as Ukranian-Dorian, is analyzed in **PART III**; "bright" and "dark" vocal qualities are explained in **PART IV**).

EXAMPLE 4.3d gives EST neume motifs for the 4.3c-passage in brackets, should readers of EST prefer rendering the text in a less imaginative way.

Neume Motifs in Yiddish Folk Song

Sixteen of the 39 *Misinai* Tunes in Appendix C are from the Lithuanian tradition of Bible chant, 12 are from German tradition, three overlap Lithuanian and German, and eight are from other traditions. The high proportion (49 percent) of the Lithuanian tradition is significant. It reveals the continuing ascendancy of Eastern Ashkenazic folkways[17] ever since the 12th century, when Rhineland communities migrated east, bringing with them their language—a mixture of German and Hebrew—and their Scripture reading, a mixture of ancient Judean and medieval German folk elements.

Over the next 200 years, Slavic entered the language of the Rhineland emigrants, transforming it into the Yiddish spoken today by Jews of Eastern Ashkenazic descent.[18] During the same period (13th-14th centuries), Rhineland neume motifs—in the form of *Misinai* Tunes—penetrated an established Synagogue-song repertoire as well as an emerging literature of Yiddish folk song. One hundred years ago, a massive emigration of Eastern Ashkenazic Jews brought the sacred and secular traditions—both saturated with neume motifs—to the United States.

Certainly neume motifs do not dominate the pieces in which they appear; they are used almost subliminally, in passing. Hence the average worshipper in America cannot discern neume motifs when adapted by the cantor for prayer (such as in *Hashkiveinu*, Example 3.9b). Even less can the average listener perceive them in Yiddish folk song. So thoroughly have they been absorbed in secular music that even Abraham Idelsohn—the world-famous Jewish ethnomusicologist—missed them, according to Cantor Max Wohlberg.[19]

A cursory examination of any Yiddish folk-song anthology confirms Wohlberg's contention. It seems no mere coincidence that so many Yiddish folk song phrases are similar to neume motifs. EXAMPLE 4.4 takes six phrases from a 1972 song collection[20] and matches them to neume motifs for the six Liturgical occasions when Scripture is read publicly (see the introduction to Appendix B for a key to abbreviations).[21]

EXAMPLE 4.4a, Black Cherries (*Shvartze Karshelech*),[22] derives from ^Lith^TOR *géireish* (see Appendix B, line I TOR, Additional-separator motif 8.b.). EXAMPLE 4.4b, Oh Far, Far Away (*Oi, Dorten, Dorten*),[23] derives from ^Lith^HAF *tipcha* (see Appendix B, line II HAF, Etnachta-group motif 2.b). EXAMPLE 4.4c, I Don't Want To Go To Religious School (*Ich Vil Nit Gehn In Cheider*),[24] derives from ^Lith^HHD *mahpach* and *zarka* (see Appendix B, line III HHD, Katon-group motif 4 and Segol-

EXAMPLE 4.4
Six Yiddish folk-song phrases, with Lithuanian neume-motif sources
from the six Scripture-reading occasions.

group motif 3.b). EXAMPLE 4.4d, Paper Is White (*Papir Iz Doch Vais*),[25] derives from ^{Lith}RES *pashtà* and $_<$ *yetiv* (see Appendix B, line IV RES, Katon-group motif 4.b and Additional-separator motif 8.f). EXAMPLE 4.4e, Little Jacob (*Yankele*),[26] derives from ^{Lith}LAM *gedolah* (see Appendix B, line V LAM, Additional-separator motif 8.e). EXAMPLE 4.4f, Song of the Baby Sitter (*Zolst Azoi Leben*),[27] derives from ^{Lith}EST *gadŏl* (see Appendix B, line VI EST, Katon-group motif 4.e).

Tracking Two Linked Neume Motifs

In this subsection we will track two representative neume motifs from the Middle East where they began, in their more recent wanderings across Europe and in the United States. Calling these two linked motifs the heart of a universal TOR/RES tradition, Abraham Idelsohn documents their continued use at the turn of this century in TOR or RES reading of 15 diaspora communities, and in the transcribed TOR tradition of a 16th community at the turn of the 16th century.[28]

The 16 diaspora communities apply Idelsohn's two linked motifs—in whole or in part—to all six of Rosowsky's neume groups (Example 3.4 and Appendix B), in the following proportions:

> Three communities (19 percent) apply them to the Rev'ia neume group.
> Four communities (25 percent) apply them to the Katon neume group.
> Five communities (31 percent) apply them to the Etnachta neume group.
> Six communities (38 percent) apply them to the Segol neume group.
> Eight communities (50 percent) apply them to the Tevir neume group.

Counting every overlap, there are 33 applications of the two linked motifs. Since the largest number of communities use them for the Tevir neume group in its essential form (*darga tevir*, see Example 3.4, neume group 6.), that is how they appear as first Parallel to *Misinai* Tune [21] in Appendix C (right-hand column), and also as EXAMPLE 4.5a.

In 1877 in Germany, the universal TOR/RES *darga tevir* motifs emerged as the opening phrase in Abraham Baer's setting of the Piyyut, *Berach, Dodi*, sung during Shacharit on Pesach (after Song of Solomon, 8:14).

Berach, dodi, udemeh lecha litsvi . . .
'Make haste, my beloved, and be like a
gazelle (EXAMPLE 4.5b).[29]

A Piyyut of the *Zulat / Ge'ulah*-type (see Example 3.11, Prayer-type –
i–'Concerning "Redemption" '), *Berach, Dodi* is given as Primary Occurrence for *Misinai* Tune 21 in Appendix C (left-hand column).

In 1882, in Berlin, the universal TOR/RES *darga tevir* motifs appeared elsewhere in the liturgy, as the recurring climax in Louis
Lewandowsky's choral setting of the Rosh Hashanah Musaf *Zichronot* or
'Remembrance' prayer, *Zacharti Lach . . .*('I remember the devotion of
your youth . . . how you followed me in the wilderness'; Jeremiah 2:2).
The two linked motifs enter as the first Recurrence of *Misinai* Tune 21
in Appendix C, middle column at the words:

be'erets lo zeru'ah
'in a land not sown'
(EXAMPLE 4.5c).[30]

In Vienna of 1905, Joseph Sulzer, Imperial Court cellist and son of the
great cantor, Salomon Sulzer, reissued his father's liturgical compositions, plus many never published before. Among the latter is the
Mechayeh-type Piyyut for Pesach Musaf, *Tal*, or Prayer for Dew (see
Prayer-type –l–, 'Concerning "Resurrection" ', in Example 3.11). Its final
strophe opens with words which Sulzer sets to the universal TOR/RES
darga tevir motifs. (See the second Recurrence of *Misinai* Tune 21 in
Appendix C, second column).

Tal bo tevareich mazon
'Bless our sustenance with dew'
(EXAMPLE 4.5d).[31]

Somewhat later, in 1932, Abraham Idelsohn included his own discovery—unknowingly and in altered form—in his catalogue of Eastern
Ashkenazic folk tunes. The universal TOR/RES *darga tevir* motifs appear as the refrain of a meditative Chasidic song, *A Dudeleh* ('Thou,
Thou'). The song is attributed to the Chasidic master, Levi Yitzchok
(1740–1810) of the Ukranian city, Berdichev. Levi Yitzchok was famous
for his ongoing argument with God about the lowly status of His 'chosen'
people, the Jews, vis-a-vis the high estate of the Gentiles. In the song's
refrain, Levi Yitzchok addresses God directly:

Oi! mizroch du, maariv du,
tsofen du, dorem du,

'Ah! Thou are east, thou are west,
thou are north, thou are south'
(EXAMPLE 4.5e).[32]

Two notes, A and G, are moved upward to A♯ and G♯ (notated as B♭
and A♭ in Example 4.5e), matching Chasidic preference for the Oriental
mode known as *Ahavah Rabah* (the Synagogue equivalent of Arabic

EXAMPLE 4.5
Tracking two linked neume motifs.

Makam Hijaz, both defined in **PART III**). These notes, plus the initial upbeat C̲, together with the ultimate sequence E̲–C̲♯–C̲♮, camouflage what is actually the heart of our original Example (4.5a): univeral TOR/RES *darga tevir*.

We can see this in Example 4.5f, the Chasidic refrain of Example 4.5e with alterations and extraneous notes removed. A Sabbath hymn, the *Keva* prayer, *Yismechu* ('They that keep the Sabbath shall rejoice') typifies the songs taught school children during the early years of Jewish resettlement in Palestine following World War I. One of the most beloved teachers at the Gymnasium Herzliah in Tel Aviv, Chanina Krachevsky, set the words of *Yismechu* to music as shown in EXAMPLE 4.5g,[33] echoing the modified Chasidic refrain of Example 4.5e. Published posthumously in 1932, Krachevsky's *Yismechu* soon became a common congregational anthem in American synagogues.

Krachevsky added flats to two notes, A̲ and D̲, to fit the universal TOR/RES *darga tevir* motifs into the Oriental mode of Example 4.5e. If we remove the flats, along with passing tones inserted to maintain a $\frac{2}{4}$ meter (see EXAMPLE 4.5h), we come closer to the Pesach-Shacharit Piyyut of Example 4.5b (*Berach Dodi*).

Neume Motifs in the Theater

Motifs that have entered the Yiddish theater are even harder to trace back to Biblical chant than motifs that have entered prayer and folk songs. But we can identify some. The early operettas of Abraham Goldfaden (1840–1908), called the 'father' of Yiddish theater, portrayed Jewish life in Eastern Europe. When Goldfaden discovered his characters (*Schmendrick* the ne'er-do-well, *Kuni-lemel* the fool) entering Jewish folklore, he broadened his horizons to write epic operettas based on Biblical tales. For one of these, *Shulamis; or The Daughter of Jerusalem* (1880), he made a lullaby, derived from a traditional folk song, the most popular Yiddish ballad ever written.

A Judean maiden, Shulamis, waits for her betrothed, Avsholom, to return and marry her. Feigning madness to ward off other suitors, she compares her plight to the widowed Daughter of Zion (the Prophet Isaiah's favorite term for Israel abandoned) in the lullaby, *Rojinkes Mit Mandlen* ('Raisins and Almonds').

> In the Holy Temple, in a little corner,
> sits the Daughter of Zion, widowed, alone.

EXAMPLE 4.6a[34] is the lullaby's second phrase,

in a vinkel cheider

'in a little corner'.

Its aura of antiquity comes from *munach katón* of [Lith]RES, EXAMPLE 4.6b[35] (see Appendix B, line IV RES, Katon-group motifs 4.c and 4.d).

Since then, cantors have regularly used *munach katón* (the key phrase of Goldfaden's lullaby) in Eastern Ashkenazic-style prayer for the second half-verse in Shabbat Shacharit, as shown in EXAMPLE 4.8c. This version, taken from Gershon Ephros' *Cantorial Anthology* (1929–1977), is credited to the Russian cantor, Abraham Ber Birnbaum (1865–1922):[36]

Shochein ad, marom vekadesh shemo

'The One who inhabits eternity, Exalted One,
whose name is holy'
(after Isaiah 57:15).

a. Second phrase of lullaby
b. *Lith* RES neume motifs
c. Second half-verse of Sabbath Shacharit

EXAMPLE 4.6
Neume motifs in a lullaby from the operetta, *Shulamis*.

Actor-producer Maurice Schwartz featured a Chasidic Nigun (word-less melody sung by the pious as a form of prayer) in his production of Sholom Asch's *Der Tehillim Yid* ('The Psalm-saying Jew'),[37] for New York's Yiddish Art Theater in 1940. In the first act, a small Chasidic community waits in vain for Elijah the Prophet, harbinger of the Messiah, as Sabbath departs and workaday cares resume. Composer Sholom Secunda set the scene to a Nigun combining yearning for the Messiah with the consolation of God's presence every Sabbath.

Secunda's Nigun begins as in EXAMPLE 4.7a,[38] employing filler-syllables, here used to express longing: *ai-bai*; *yababa-bam*; etc. The arching melody—up a fifth and down again—here shows acceptance of the 'widowed-Daughter-of-Zion' state, following musicologist Deryck Cooke's guidelines. (A phrase in minor which ascends to its fifth degree and descends again to its tonic expresses a sorrowful yielding to misfortune.)[39] The melody itself can be traced to various [Lith]HAF neume motifs cited in EXAMPLE 4.7b.[40]

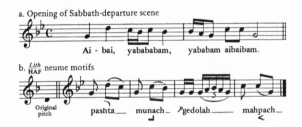

EXAMPLE 4.7
Neume motifs in first act of *Der Tehillim Yid*.

Neume Motifs in a Wedding March

To bring the 'widowed-Daughter-of-Zion' music of Goldfaden (Example 4.6a) and Secunda (Example 4.7a) to its logical cadence, we analyze a Chasidic wedding march, *Od Yishama* ('Let There Again Be Heard'). The words are taken from the final benediction of the traditional Jewish wedding liturgy:

> Let there again be heard—in the cities of Judah and in the
> streets of Jerusalem—the voice of joy and gladness, the
> voice of bride and groom (after Jeremiah 33:10–11).

EXAMPLE 4.8a[41] is in G minor (like the *Tehillim Yid*-theme of Example 4.7a), but rises only to the third degree (B♭) rather than to the fifth (D). This, says Deryck Cooke, reveals a "feeling of courage," while its subsequent fall to the minor tonic (G) discloses an "acceptance of grief."[42] How so? The Jewish wedding liturgy, formulated after the Second Temple's destruction in the year 70, already looked forward to a far-distant national restoration. The unknown Chasidic group who much later set this wedding-text to the specific melody of Example 4.8a crafted a march expressing grief over the calamity that befell Israel, and also expectance of a brighter future for coming generations; in a word: expressing acceptance.

The neume and prayer motifs underpinning the wedding-march melody also deal with grief. EXAMPLE 4.8b[43] gives the Sephardic Et-nachta-group motifs used for chanting Lamentations ([Seph]LAM) on the Eve of Tishah B'av (the Ninth of Av), a mid-summer day of mourning commemorating the sack of both Temples and numerous other catastrophes. EXAMPLE 4.8c[44] is the way Ashkenazic communities offer Maariv prayers on the same occasion:

> ... *tamid yimloch aleinu* ...
> 'The King, who in his glory will reign over us
> and over all his works forever'.

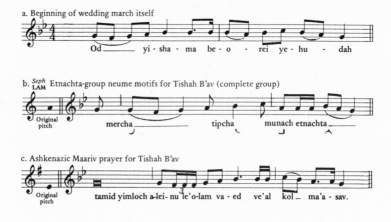

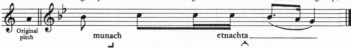

EXAMPLE 4.8
Neume motifs from Lamentations (LAM) in a Chasidic wedding march.

EXAMPLE 4.8d combines two neume motifs to form a truncated Etnachta group (*munach etnachta*) for reading LAM following Tishah B'av Maariv. The same two motifs occur in the Tishah B'av rite of every diaspora tradition, whether Sephardic, Ashkenazic, or Oriental. Of the seven LAM traditions documented by Idelsohn,[45] five (71 percent) use the two motifs as a truncated Etnachta group, enough to warrant our labeling them universal LAM motifs. The universal LAM motifs of Example 4.8d also appear in Example 4.8c, at the words *ve'al kol ma'asav* ('. . . and over all his works'), as sung for Tishah B'av Maariv in both Eastern and Western Ashkenazic communities.

Jewish dreams were ever articulated in the neume motifs of Biblical chant, kernels of melody that have linked epochs together. In the words of historian Michael Horovitz, they have stirred "the echoes of ancestral lamentations . . . tracing back . . . to the Piyyut and Ecclesiastes."[46] The faces of neumes may change; regional folk song and vocal preference may alter their intervals and pitch. They may be dramatized, quoted in folk song or folk dance, sung—in sorrow or joy—in prayer or on stage. Whatever their end use, the more closely neume motifs approach their origins, the more miraculously do they transport their listeners back to God's world as Scripture tells us it was

In the beginning (Genesis 1:1).

The Many Faces of Neume Motifs: Bibliography & Notes

1. ROSOWSKY, Solomon: "Theater and Art," Preface to *Jacob and Rachel*, Tel Aviv, Ha'Ohel (1925), pages 6–7.
2. BOESCHENSTEIN, Johannes: Transcription of [Ger]TOR neume motifs, in Johannes Reuchlin's *De Accentibus et Orthographia Linguae Hebraicae*, Hagenau (1518); charted by COHEN, Francis Lyon: "Cantillation," *Jewish Encyclopedia,* New York, Funk & Wagnalls (1903), Volume 3:540–549, line 1.b, throughout.
3. MAYEROWITSCH, H., and G. Prince: "Cantillation for the Reading of the Torah and Prophets," *The Pentateuch and Haphtorahs*, edited by J.H. Hertz, London, Soncino, Second edition (1962), pages 1045–1046.

4. LEVINE, Joseph A.: *Emunat Abba* (Baltimore Hebrew College, 1981), Ann Arbor, University Microfilms, Volume II, pages 281–284.
5. ROSOWSKY, Solomon: *The Cantillation of the Bible*, New York, Reconstructionist (1957), pages 606–613.
6. VINAVER, Chemjo: *Anthology of Jewish Music*, New York, Marks (1955), pages 23–27.
7. YASSER, Joseph: "How Can the Ancient Hebrew Melos Be Restored?" *Cantors Assembly Proceedings* (1956), 9:30.
8. HOHENEMSER, Jacob: Cantor and musicologist, in a letter to Joseph A. Levine, *South German Chazanut*, Providence (May 28, 1962).
9. WERNER, Eric: *A Voice Still Heard*, University Park, Pennsylvania State University (1976), page 219.
10. HERBERT-CAESARI, E.: *Vocal Truth*, London, Robert Hale (1969), page 70.
11. LEWANDOWSKY, Louis: *Kol Rinnah Ut'fillah*, Berlin, published by the author (1871), number 54.
12. ALMAN, Samuel: *Synagogue Compositions*, Part I, Berlin, Juwal (1925), number 46.
13. LEVINE (see item 4), Volume II, number 364.
14. NE'EMAN, Yehoshua Leib: *Nosach Lachazan*, Jerusalem, Israel Institute (1969), page 106.
15. KOUSSEVITSKY, Moshe: *From the Repertoire of Cantor Moshe Koussevitsky*, New York, Tara (1977), page 22.
16. WEISGAL, Abba Yosef: *Purim Eve Service*, private recording, Baltimore, Chizuk Amuno Synagogue (March 20, 1962), transcribed by Joseph A. Levine.
17. DUKER, Abraham G.: " Emerging Cultural Patterns in American Jewish Life," *Publications of the American Jewish Historical Society* (1949–1950), Volume 39, pages 351–388.
18. DAVIDOWICZ, Lucy: *The Jewish Presence*, New York, Rhinehart (1977), page 157.
19. WOHLBERG, Max: "The Music of the Synagogue as Source of the Yiddish Folksong," *Musica Judaica*, New York, American Society for Jewish Music, Volume II (1977–1978), page 21.
20. MLOTEK, Eleanor Gordon: *The New Book of Yiddish Songs*, New York, Workmen's Circle (1972).
21. ROSOWSKY, Solomon: *Neume Motifs for the Yearly Cycle of Biblical Chant According to the Lithuanian Tradition*, after manuscripts, New York, Jewish Theological Seminary (1958); Appendix B.
22. BLACK CHERRIES: (Cahan, 1912; see item 20), page 29.
23. OH, FAR, FAR AWAY: (Ginzburg & Marek, 1901; see item 20), page 27.
24. I DON'T WANT TO GO TO RELIGIOUS SCHOOL: (Cherniawsky, circa 1910; see item 20), page 13.
25. PAPER IS WHITE: (Cahan, 1912; see item 20), page 20.
26. LITTLE JACOB: (Gebirtig, circa 1920; see item 20), page 8.
27. SONG OF THE BABY SITTER: (Cahan, 1928; see item 20), page 11.

6666666666666666666

66666666

28. IDELSOHN, Abraham Zvi: *Toledot Haneginah Ha'ivrit*, Tel Aviv, Dvir (1924), pages 118-141, 192; the 15 early-20th century communities are: Babylonia; Bukhara; Syria; Morocco; Gibraltar; France; Italy; Amsterdam; London; Egypt; Balkans; Salonika; Germany; Lithuania; and Carpentras. The early-16th century community is Hagenau (in the Rhineland).

29. BAER, Abraham: *Baal T'fillah*, Gothenburg, published by the author (1877), number 788a.

30. LEWANDOWSKY, Louis: *Todah W'simrah*, Berlin, published by the author, Volume II (1882), number 198.

31. SULZER, Salomon: *Schir Zion* (Vienna, 1839–1865), revised by Joseph Sulzer, Vienna (1905), number 249.

32. IDELSOHN, Abraham Zvi: "The Folk Song of the East European Jews," *Thesaurus of Hebrew Oriental Melodies*, Volume IX, Leipzig, Hofmeister (1932), number 125.

33. KRACHEVSKY, Chanina: *Tselilei Chanina*, Tel Aviv, Herzlia (1932), number 43.

34. GOLDFADEN, Abraham: *Rojinkes Mit Mandlen* (1880), arranged by Zavel Zilbersts, New York, Metro (1962), page 2.

35. ROSOWSKY (see item 21), Appendix B, line IV RES, motifs 4.c and 4.d.

36. EPHROS, Gershon: "Shabbat," *Cantorial Anthology*, New York, Bloch (1953), Volume IV, page 196.

37. ASCH, Scholom: *Der Tehillim Yid*, New York, Morning Freiheit Association (1936).

38. SECUNDA, Sholom: *Nigun Und Havdoloh*, New York, Metro (1940), page 2.

39. COOKE, Deryck: *The Language of Music*, London, Oxford (1959), pages 107; 133.

40. ROSOWSKY (see item 21), Appendix B, line II HAF, motifs: 4.b; 7.b; 8.e; and 4.a.

41. PASTERNAK, Velvel: *Songs of the Chasidim*, New York, Bloch (1968), Volume I, number 154.

42. COOKE: (see item 39), pages 125–126; 133.

43. IDELSOHN (see item 28), page 193: LAM, line 5, final neume group.

44. BAER (see item 29), number 166a.

45. IDELSOHN (see item 28), page 193, LAM. The seven traditions cited are: Yemenite; Iranian; Iraqi; Syrian; Eastern Sephardic; Western Sephardic; Ashkenazic.

46. HOROVITZ, Michael: "Judaism, the Mid-century, and Me," *Next Year in Jerusalem*, edited by Douglas Villiers, New York, Viking (1976), pages 113–114.

PART III

MODAL TECHNIQUE

*Know that Jacob our father sent his
ten sons to their brother Joseph in Egypt
with the musical modes of the land of Israel.
This is the hidden meaning of the verse,
"Take of the choice fruits of the land
(mizimrat ha'arets) in your bags"
(Genesis 43:11), for zimrah also means 'song'.*

"Nachman of Braslav on Song,"
Hillel Zeitlin,
Lachasidim Mizmor, 1935
M. Geshuri

CHAPTER FIVE

Defining the Three Principal Prayer Modes

A s their Latin root *modus* ('manner') implies, Prayer modes are ways or fashions of chanting prayer. The three Principal Prayer modes are: *Adonai Malach* ('The Lord Reigns'); *Magein Avot* ('Our Forbears' Shield'); and *Ahavah Rabah* ('With Abounding Love'). This chapter shows how the Principal Prayer modes combine Psalmodic technique with Biblical technique while governing the intervallic spacing of both. It delves into the modes' origins, explains their individual characteristics, and illustrates their use in the liturgy of American synagogues.

The Third Synagogue–song Component

Modal chant—the norm for most cantors—is musically more interesting than either Psalmodic or Biblical chant. Like singers of traditional Oriental (Non-Occidental) music, a cantor chanting prayers concentrates on the melodic line, selecting from a stock of prescribed motifs, bridging them through reciting-tones and melismatic flourishes. Each cantor varies the selection of motifs, their rhythm, intervallic spacing, and how the notes sound. Flexibility comes foremost. Prayer modes may be varied endlessly, limited only by the cantor's imagination, yet they are always recognizable. Hence a Prayer mode is a sacred vocal pattern of traditional motifs that retains its identity even though melody, rhythm, and note-intervals and note-sequences change, according to where in the liturgy the prayer is sung. EXAMPLE 5.1,[1] although the text is Scriptural, appears as a prayer (in the Selichot, or 'Penitential' service inaugurating the High Holy Days), and is not treated as Bible reading.

Im yihyu chata'eichem kashanim . . .
'Though your sins are like scarlet, they shall
be white as snow' (Isaiah 1:18).

EXAMPLE 5.1.
Psalmodic Reciting-tones combined with Biblical neume-like motifs.

In Example 5.1, Psalmodic chant contributes the syllabic reciting-tones while Biblical chant supplies the neume-like motifs. The result balances Psalmodic rapidity with Biblical deliberateness.

Either half of Example 5.1, for instance, lasts about seven seconds sung at *mp* or *mf*. Readers may vary their interpretation, lengthening and shortening note values, or raising and lowering volume. The object is to heighten the verse's parallelism through combinations of the chant-techniques learned thus far. (Compare Example 3.2, also a Scriptural text used in prayer. The Psalmodic pattern of 3.2a is sung rapidly in five seconds at *mp*; the Biblical pattern of 3.2b is sung deliberately in nine seconds at *mf*).

EXAMPLE 5.2[2] by Pierre Pinchik (1897–1971), clearly reveals artistry in a Prayer mode. EXAMPLE 5.2a opens with two reciting-tones, both on B♭. These contrast with the neume-like motifs of EXAMPLE 5.2b (resembling Haftarah *segol* and *reviʻa*), and EXAMPLE 5.2c (resembling High Holy Day *yetiv* and *munach*; the *munach* carried through a descending run of 13 notes on the word, *shabbat*). EXAMPLE 5.2d extends High Holy Day *yetiv* and *munach* further, into an elaborate melismatic passage which climaxes on a *ppp* high F. The *munach*-motif is fragmented, beginning at *olmin* and concluding at the final *bar minah*. This perfectly tone-paints the text, *Raza Deshabbat* ('The Essence of Sabbath'), a mystical Aramaic preamble to Friday Evening Maariv, proclaiming the Sabbath's dominion over all harsh decrees.

> *veleit shultana achara belchulhu olmin,*
> *bar minah*
>
> 'and no other power reigns in all the world,
> except the Sabbath'.

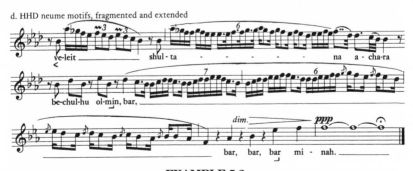

EXAMPLE 5.2
Pinchik's *Raza Deshabbat*: artistry in a Prayer mode.

Comparing Prayer Modes with
Musical Scales and Arabic *Makamat*

Late-19th and early-20th century researchers Josef Singer in Vienna,[3] Alois Kaiser and William Sparger in Chicago,[4] and Francis Cohen in London[5] incorrectly compared Prayer modes to musical scales. They are easier to understand as models "demonstrating typical movements (motifs) within a scalar framework."[6] Later historians Hyman Harris[7] and Alfred Sendrey,[8] both in New York, as well as sociologist Samuel Heilman[9] in Chicago, applied the term *nusach* to Prayer modes, following mid-20th century American chazanic parlance. But *nusach* really connotes a textual formula—as in *Nusach Ashkenaz* or *Nusach Sepharad*—referring to Ashkenazic or Sephardic prayer-rubrics rather than to modes of chant. Hanoch Avenary[10] finds more cause to liken Prayer modes to Middle Eastern *makamat* than to the Western European Church modes scholars favored following Hirsch Weintraub's 1859 study.[11] Most contemporary ethnomusicologists, including this author, agree with Avenary. *Makam*, singular for *makamat*, originally meant the raised platform from which Arabic singers entertained the Caliph. It now means "a pattern of melody . . . characterized by stereotype turns, by its mood, and even by its pitch."[12] Or as Johanna Spector suggests:

> Improvisation in a *makam* can be likened to . . .
> a theme with variations . . . Oriental musicians think in
> terms of melodic line, the dominant force in Middle Eastern
> music, and not in terms of harmony or polyphony and
> vertical structure, as Western musicians do. The more
> elaborate the embellishments, intervallic finesse, and
> complex rhythm of the melodic line, the more interesting
> and satisfying to the Oriental musician.[13]

Adds Alfred Sendrey, "Oriental and other 'primitive' musics boast of intervals which our 'advanced' system cannot accommodate."[14] Sendrey refers to the microtones (intervals smaller than the Western half-step) found in ethnic music everywhere except in the Post-Renaissance European tradition with its tempered scale of intervals. Critic Henry Pleasants writes:

[The European system] cannot reflect the myriad shadings
of attack, color, vibrato, release and so on that distinguish . . .
singing . . . The slight deviations from pitch and their
harmonic and melodic connotations . . . [are] rhythmic
subtleties foreign to the fractional subdivisions of time in the
rhythmic organization of European music.[15]

In Oriental, as opposed to Occidental music, solo singing is generally more important than instrumental playing, and melody generally more important than harmony. Most admired is the extended solo *tartil* (Arabic for 'recitative'; called *zogachts* in Yiddish). Here the singer pours forth his or her innermost feelings in non-metrical form. The vocal nuances of this unaccompanied song are too subtle for most Occidental audiences to detect.

Origins of the Prayer Modes

From what primordial layer of Hebraic tradition do the Prayer modes stem? Idelsohn considers them echoes of Bible reading, "though with variations and additions of motifs."[16] We saw in **PART II** that many of the neume motifs that form the basis of Bible reading in the 16 diaspora traditions analyzed by Idelsohn exhibit amazing similarity, particulary Lamentations (Example 4.8). This widespread similarity—known as 'diffusion' in ethnomusicological terminology—suggests to Idelsohn "that they were already folk-song before the destruction of the Second Temple."[17]

Scholars have equated the universal Bible chant for reading Torah with Arabic *Makam Siga*, shown in its essential form as Example 5.3a.[18] Early-diaspora cantors recognized in the *Siga*-pattern, heard throughout the Middle East, familiar elements of Pre-exilic Judean folk song. They adapted the *makam* as a ready-made formula in which to chant Torah, the mainstay of many synagogue services, (shown in its essential form as Example 5.3b).[19] The same mode next spread to the Festival reading of Ruth-Ecclesiastes-Song of Solomon (RES), and then to the *Keva* sections of an emerging prayer order (*Siddur Tefillah*). In effect, the TOR/RES mode was enlisted as a *Tefillah* ('Prayer') mode. Sephardic *chazanim* still recognize it as the *Tefillah* mode while Ashkenazic cantors call it *Adonai Malach* (after Psalm 93, 'The Lord Reigns', originally the opening prayer on Friday Night). The antecedent and consequent phrases of both *Makam Siga* (Example 5.3a) and Torah reading (Example 5.3b) share a Middle Eastern origin. The final—or tonic—of this original mode was F♯ (on the pitch level shown here, actually E in the fixed system of *makamat*). The influence of European folk song caused Ashkenazic cantors to close a third lower, creating a new tonal center. This was especially true in Southwest Germany, where the transition to Prayer mode first took place in Europe. EXAMPLE 5.3c[20] illustrates universal Ashkenazic RES reading, with its lowered final D. During the Middle Ages the same mode entered Gregorian chant—without the lowered final—and still appears in the Roman Catholic Mass as *Kyrie Eleison* ('Lord, Have Mercy') in Mode III, called Phrygian (EXAMPLE 5.3d).[21]

EXAMPLE 5.3e[22] represents the last stage by which TOR/RES reading evolved into the *Adonai Malach* Prayer mode. The antecedent phrase took on an additional motif, subdividing into opening and pause. The consequent phrase also took on an additional motif, subdividing into continuation and cadence. As with modes generally, *Adonai Malach* assumes extra-musical associations,[23] connoting regal tenderness, its mood suiting any prayer-text voicing Divine praise.[24]

EXAMPLE 5.3e[22] also gives equivalents for the four *Adonai Malach* motifs among the *Misinai* Tunes (indicated by boxed numbers; see Appendix C, left-hand column): [1], a *Barechu*-type ('Call to Prayer'); [11], an *Aleinu*-type ('Adoration'); [25], a *Mechayeh*-type ('Concerning "Resurrection" '); and [4], another *Barechu*-type.

Model of Prayer Mode, *Adonai Malach*

Each prayer mode has its own stock of motifs. The four motifs listed in Example 5.3e form a skeleton of the Ashkenazic *Adonai Malach* mode, set to the initial verse of Psalm 93, with the four skeletal-motif words (underlined):

> 1. The Lord Reigns (*Adonai Malach* [1]) ; he is robed in
> majesty; the Lord is robed (*laveish adonai* [2]), he is girded
> with strength (*oz hit'azar* [3]). Yea, the world is established;
> it shall never be moved (*bal timot* [4]).

With the four skeletal motifs (numbered [1] through [4] in EXAMPLE 5.4a), their equivalent neume-motifs (EXAMPLE 5.4b), and *Misinai* Tunes (EXAMPLE 5.4c), we begin to flesh out a model of the Prayer mode, *Adonai Malach*.

EXAMPLE 5.3

Adonai Malach: origins of a Prayer mode.

In all Examples the author appears top right. In Examples 5.4b and 5.4c, the Bible-reading tradition, *Misinai* Prayer-type, and initial liturgical Occurrences also appear top left. For details refer to Appendix C.

In Volumes I and II of his *Thesaurus* (1923–1933),[25] Idelsohn has left us two versions of *Adonai Malach*, encompassing Western and Eastern Ashkenazic practice. EXAMPLE 5.5 combines both of Idelsohn's versions to yield four additional motifs: [1a]; [2a]; [3a]; and [3b]. Each motif relates to a typical modal sequence: [1a] usually follows [1], an opening motif; [2a] often echoes [2], a motif that ends the antecedent phrase; [3a] and [3b] alternate with [3] as continuing motifs that initiate the consequent phrase. (The general contour of an antecedent and consequent phrase in *Adonai Malach*—including motifs [1], [2], and [3]—appears in Example 5.3e). The numeration of Prayer-mode motifs is my own.

EXAMPLE 5.4
Four skeletal motifs of *Adonai Malach* mode,
with neume-motif and *Misinai* Tune equivalents.

Three Different Tone Densities within a Prayer Mode

Before approaching the two other Principal Prayer modes, *Magein Avot* and *Ahavah Rabah*, readers might benefit from examining *Adonai Malach* passages in syllabic, neumatic, and melismatic tone densities. EXAMPLE 5.6a[26] is the first of many *Zemirot* (table songs) which medieval mystics added to the Sabbath Grace after meals. Simeon ben Isaac ben Abun (10th century, Mayence) composed the text, *Baruch Adonai Yom, Yom.* The head of the household intones a verse, and all present join in a response. Though stately, the Psalmodic-style syllabic chant moves at a brisk pace.

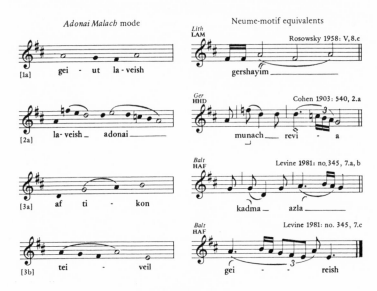

EXAMPLE 5.5

Four additional *Adonai Malach* motifs from Idelsohn's Eastern-and-Western
Ashkenazic versions, with neume-motif equivalents.

Head of household sings verse:

Blessed be the Lord, who daily
loadeth us with deliverance and redemption.
In his name we will rejoice continually;
in his salvation we will raise our head high.

All present respond:

For he is a strength to the poor
and a refuge to the needy.

EXAMPLE 5.6b,[27] from the Shabbat Musaf Kedushah, is the most
deliberate of the three Examples. The sequential repetition of each
neume-like motif in this chant tries the patience of a standing congregation. (A seated congregation hears Bible reading, where 'teaching-
through-song' normally prevails). A congregational response follows
every Kedushah-verse, just as in Example 5.6a.

Kevodo malei olam . . .

'His glory fills the universe;
his ministering angels ask one another:
"Where is the place of his glory?" '

EXAMPLE 5.6

Adonai Malach: passages in three tone densities; chart of 17 motifs.

d. Chart of 17 *Adonai Malach* motifs

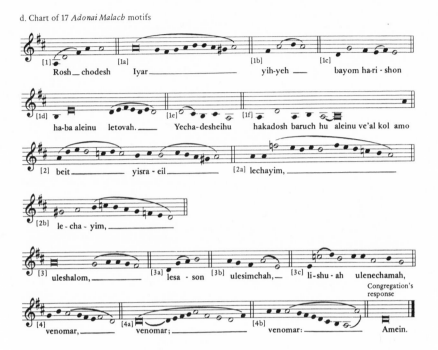

EXAMPLE 5.6, *continued.*

EXAMPLE 5.6c[28] is fourth among the Marriage service's seven benedictions (*Sheva Berachot*),

> *asher yatsar et ha'adam ...*
> '[Blessed art thou, O Lord,]
> who hast made man in thine image,
> after thy likeness,
> and hast prepared unto him
> a woman to stand beside him'.

As befits the occasion, it is effusive in praising God (as are all *Adonai Malach* passages), using melismatic flourishes as melody. Yet the ornamentation does not tire a standing bridal party nor a seated family and friends, who respond to every mention of God's name: *Baruch hu uvaruch shemo* ('Blessed be he and blessed be his name'); and to every benediction: *Amein* ('Amen'), as shown. Crisply sung repartee, affirming approval by all present, is the mark of Prayer-mode chant.

EXAMPLES 5.4 and 5.5 showed eight *Adonai Malach* motifs along with their neume-motif equivalents. EXAMPLE 5.6d includes five more motifs to be discussed later. The 17 motifs of Example 5.6b form a model for many *Adonai Malach* texts. The text given—to help readers in singing the chart—is the announcement and blessing of a New Month.

> *Rosh chodesh Iyar ... Yechadesheihu ...*
> 'The New Month of Iyar will begin on Sunday.
> May God grant that it bring to all Israel
> life and peace, gladness and joy,
> salvation and comfort, amen'.

The Didactic Mode: *Magein Avot*

The second of three Principal Prayer modes—*Magein Avot*—is contemporary with *Adonai Malach* but stems from Haftarah rather than Torah reading. Its Middle Eastern *makam*-equivalent is a blend of two *makamat*: *Bayat*, the most widespread *makam* (stressing $\underline{D}$); and *Bayat-Nava* (stressing $\underline{G}$). EXAMPLE 5.7a[29] gives six typical phrases of the combined *makam*. Parallels for the six *makam*-phrases occur in various diaspora Haftarah-traditions. EXAMPLE 5.7b[30] offers neume motifs from three: Lithuanian ([Lith]), Babylonian ([Bab]), and Ashkenazic ([Ash]), which join to form a hypothetical Prayer-mode equivalent to the combined *makam* of Example 5.7a.

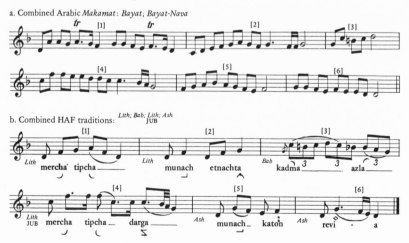

EXAMPLE 5.7
Middle Eastern equivalents of, and Biblical parallels for, *Magein Avot* mode.

EXAMPLE 5.8a[31]shows how 19th-century cantor-compiler Abraham Baer used the Prayer mode to sing the text after which it is named, *Magein Avot*. The third of four paragraphs summarizing the silent Friday Night Amidah just concluded, *Magein Avot* teaches the relevance of Sabbath observance:

EXAMPLE 5.8
Magein Avot motifs.

b. Charted in sequence

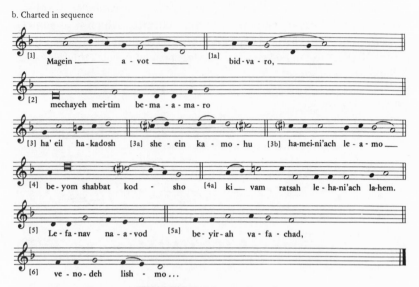

EXAMPLE 5.8, *continued.*

> *Magein Avot bidvaro, mechayeh meitim
> bema'amaro . . .*
>
> 'Our forbears' shield, reviver of the dead,
> incomparable God . . . We serve him in awe,
> daily blessing his name, God deserving of
> thanks,
> Lord of peace who hallows the seventh day,
> giving Sabbath-rest to a joyful people,
> in remembrance of Creation'.

Notice how Baer chooses a different sequence of *Magein Avot* motifs from the sequence shown in Example 5.7: [1]; [3]; [5]; [3a] (an extension of [3]); and [4]. He also shapes them differently than in the combined-*makam* or combined-Haftarah parallels of Example 5.7. Motif [1], for instance, here resembles Moroccan Haftarah ([Mor]HAF) *munach katòn* rather than [Lith]HAF *mercha tipcha* as in Example 5.7b. The five motifs unique to Example 5.7a are: [1a]; [3a]; [3b]; [4b]; and [5a].

EXAMPLE 5.8b charts the 11 motifs of the *Magein Avot* mode introduced thus far, in sequence. It uses the first half of the prayer, *Magein Avot*, quoted above, as chart-text.

The liturgical section in which Example 5.8 appears, sung entirely in *Magein Avot*, connects Creation with the Sabbath. Beginning with *Vaichulu Hashamayim* . . . ('Thus the heavens and the earth were finished'; Genesis 2:1), continuing through the benediction *Koneh Shamayim Va'arets* ('Master of Heaven and Earth') and the *Magein Avot* paragraph cited in Example 5.8, the section concludes with *Retseh* ('Accept Our Rest'), which advances work-abstinence as an opportunity for studying God's Law.

Eloheinu veilohei avoteinu, retseh
vimnuchateinu . . .
'Our God and God of our forbears,
accept our rest;
hallow us through thy commandments
and grant our portion in thy law . . .
Purify our hearts to serve thee in truth'.

EXAMPLE 5.9 demonstrates three different tone densities for chanting *Eloheinu . . . Retseh* within *Magein Avot*. Psalmodic EXAMPLE 5.9a,[32] after the Chasidic tradition of Warka, Poland, is syllabic. Neumatic EXAMPLE 5.9b,[33] by the turn-of-the-century Russian cantor, Abraham Kalechnik, is more deliberate, imitating Biblical technique. Melismatic EXAMPLE 5.9c,[34] by the gifted American lyric tenor, Joseph Shlisky (1894–1955), though inspired by neume motifs embedded in its listeners' collective memory, is a vocal *tour de force*. Its sustained half-notes and sweeping cadenzas compellingly show how *Magein Avot*, the Didactic mode, teaches a religious truth.

Cantors habitually take license with Prayer-mode motifs, shaping them to fit a preferred style. Thus the motifs in Example 5.9a are squeezed horizontally to give the effect of reciting-tones. The neume-like motifs of Example 5.9b are sung with near-Biblical precision. Example 5.9c extends the modal material—through coloratura—until it is almost unrecognizable. Most motifs in Examples 5.9a, 5.9b, and 5.9c relate to the chart in Example 5.8b. Four new motifs are: [2a]; [3c]; [4b]; and [5b].

EXAMPLE 5.9d is a composite chart of 16 *Magein Avot* motifs, adding motif [2b] (shown later in Example 6.3a), to the four new ones.

EXAMPLE 5.9

Magein Avot: passages in three different tone densities; chart of 16 motifs.

d. Chart of 16 *Magein Avot* motifs

EXAMPLE 5.9, *continued.*

The Mode of Supplication: *Ahavah Rabah*

How strange that *Ahavah Rabah*, used to plead for God's mercy,[35] is the only Principal Prayer mode not rooted in Biblical chant (*Adonai Malach* stems from TOR, *Magein Avot* stems from HAF). How strange, too, that while the two other Principal Prayer modes employ diatonic (whole-and-half) steps exclusively, *Ahavah Rabah* relies on the augmented-second interval (E♭–F♯ in our musical Examples), like the Arabic *Makam Hijaz*. EXAMPLE 5.10a[36] shows one such usage of *Makam Hijaz*, the Call to Prayer of the muezzin, the Muslim equivalent of a town crier. The muezzin call builds on five motifs: [1]; [1a]; [2]; [3]; and [3a].

> *Allahu akbar . . .*
> 'Alla is great,
> there is no God beside Alla,
> and Mohammed is the messenger of Alla.
> Hasten to prayer,
> hasten to service!'

Similarities between *Makam Hijaz* and the *Ahavah Rabah* mode are self-evident in EXAMPLE 5.10b,[37] Idelsohn's transcription of an Eastern European Atonement prayer from Neilah, quoting Exodus 34:6–7. The Atonement prayer recalls three *Makam Hijaz* motifs: [2]; [3]; and [3a], while adding one new motif, [4].

> *6. Adonai, adonai . . .*
> 'The Lord, the Lord, a God merciful and
> gracious,
> slow to anger, and abounding
> in steadfast love and faithfulness,
> 7. keeping steadfast love for thousands,
> forgiving iniquity and transgression and sin,
> but who will by no means clear the guilty . . .
> pardon our iniquity and sin, and make us thy
> very own'.

EXAMPLE 5.10c combines the above-listed motifs with two others: *Makam Hijaz* motifs [1] and [1a], to set the Supplicatory mode's primary text, from Shacharit:

Ahavah rabah ahavtanu . . .

'With abounding love hast thou loved us, O
God, great mercy hast thou bestowed upon us'.

EXAMPLE 5.10
Makam Hijaz and *Ahavah Rabah* parallels.

c. Six *Makam Hijaz* motifs set to text of *Ahavah Rabah*

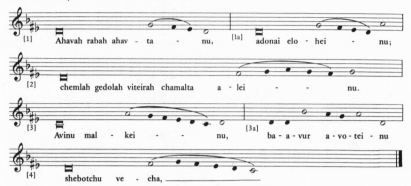

EXAMPLE 5.10, *continued.*

True, the mode we call *Ahavah Rabah* flourished in ancient Israel, chiefly as accompaniment for the bloody, Phoenician-inspired Baal-rites. Played on the double-piped *abuv* (equated with *chalil* in Babylonian Talmud, tractate *Arachin* 10b), which was tuned to accommodate the mode's augmented-second interval, *Ahavah Rabah* evidently was never heard in the First Temple and only sparingly in the Second Temple.[38] Thus it was never included in Scripture reading, as it doesn't appear in the oldest diaspora Psalmodic or Biblical traditions. Nor is it known in 20th-century usage of Yemenite, Lithuanian, Iraqi, Italian, or Moroccan Jews.[39] Why, then, was it adopted by exilic Jewish communities living in predominantly Tatar environments during the 13th century? The explanation would seem to parallel the adaptation by early-diaspora cantors of the *makam, Siga,* a millenium before; *Hijaz* recalled—even peripherally—the legacy of a proud national past. At one time rejected, the *Ahavah Rabah* mode became an avenue of supplication to God in perilous times.

No longer a proud and sovereign people but weak and oppressed, East European Jews living in the Balkans, Hungary, Rumania, the Ukraine, and Volhynia welcomed *Ahavah Rabah* as a vehicle for petitioning God. In Cantor Edward Berman's view, "they exploited the emotional power of that mode so that it served noble, albeit intense emotions. Thus,*Hijaz* served to maintain the Middle Eastern character of East European *chazanut.*"[40]

Ahavah Rabah has since been cherished by the Jewish folk as no other mode,[41] a phenomenon to which at least two musicologists have objected on the grounds of illegitimacy.[42] But, maintains cantor and scholar Leib Glantz, "whatever its birth . . . the *Ahavah Rabah* mode has become a love child of the family of Jewish Prayer chant."[43]

Reservations about *Ahavah Rabah* are better directed at its lack of musical definition, especially in the liturgical sections where it traditionally predominates, such as Shabbat Shacharit and Musaf. One searches in vain through the published literature for any hint of Biblical neume-motif contour. It is because *Ahavah Rabah* outwardly follows the pattern of *Makam Hijaz*, limiting itself—as in Example 5.10—to a few recurrent phrases within the tonal range of a fifth or sixth.

One way of skirting this limitation is to repeat melodic ideas at a different pitch level, a typically Eastern European device.[44] Usage may vary for the occasion, with the lower-pitched motifs used on weekdays and higher, more florid passages used for Shabbat. Idelsohn provides a working model from Shabbat Shacharit, using *Ahavah Rabah* on D̲ and A̲), in alternation (EXAMPLE 5.11a).[45]

> *Al harishonim ve'al ha'acharonim . . .*
> 'Alike for former and later ages, thy work is
> good and valid forever; true and trustworthy,
> a law that shall not pass away!'

The initial motif is new: [1b]; on D̲. It is followed by motif [3], suddenly on A̲, the same mode, but a fifth higher in pitch. Line two combines D̲–motif [1b] with new motif [3a] on A̲. In line three, new motif [3a]—on A̲—moves down, joining motif [1] on D̲. The syllables *oi vei*, expressive of longing (compare Example 4.7a), enter as motif [1] on D̲. They continue as: [4] on A̲; [1] on D̲; and an extended [3] on A̲, ending with the words *ve'al ha'acharonim.*

EXAMPLE 5.11b adds two new motifs—[1b] and [3a]—to our growing modal outline, using the words of *Al Harishonim*. It also suggests possible Biblical underpinning for the *Ahavah Rabah* motifs, which resemble neume motifs in general contour but not in specific intervals. Compare the *Ahavah Rabah* motifs on the left with their Biblical neume-motif cross-references on the right (drawn from Appendix B). The unknown composer of Example 5.11a evidently had neumes in mind, judging from the conventional way he grouped his figurations. The absolute pitches of neume motifs vary by Scriptural book and

EXAMPLE 5.11

Al Harishonim: sung in *Ahavah Rabah* on two alternate pitch levels;
shown as chart of *Ahavah Rabah* motifs.

liturgical occasion.[46] When they are alluded to in prayer, their absolute pitches also vary by mode. Thus the pitch-differences between *Ahavah Rabah* motifs in Example 5.11b and their neume-motif cross-references are due to the fact that their Prayer mode is almost nonexistent in Bible reading.

One must first train the eye to strip away pitch alterations, and train the ear to recognize note figurations. Neume motifs will then emerge from even the most complex Prayer-mode chant. EXAMPLE 5.12 gives three *Ahavah Rabah* mode realizations of the Sabbath Morning Priestly Blessing (Numbers 6:24–26),

> *Eloheinu . . . borcheinu vabrachah*
> *hamshuleshet . . .*
> 'Our God and God of our forbears, bless us
> with the three-fold benediction, written in the
> Torah by Moses thy servant and spoken by
> Aaron and his Priestly sons, thusly:'.

As in Examples 5.6 and 5.9, the three Priestly-blessing realizations use three tone densities: syllabic (EXAMPLE 5.12a);[47] neumatic (EXAMPLE 5.12b);[48] and melismatic (EXAMPLE 5.12c).[49] EXAMPLE 5.12d summarizes the 11 *Ahavah Rabah* motifs shown thus far. It includes the three new ones appearing in Examples 5.12a, 5.12b, and 5.12c: [1c]; [1d]; and [2a], and extends all previous motifs to reflect typical cantorial usage. One additional motif, [2b], listed last of all, represents a modal change and is discussed elsewhere (Example 6.3b). Since it completes the *Ahavah Rabah* mode, it appears here as well.

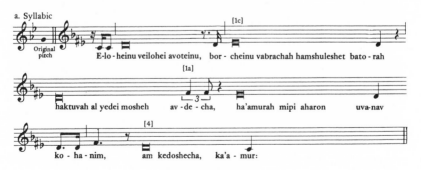

EXAMPLE 5.12

Ahavah Rabah: passages in three tone densities; chart of 11 motifs.

d. Chart of 11 *Ahavah Rabah* motifs

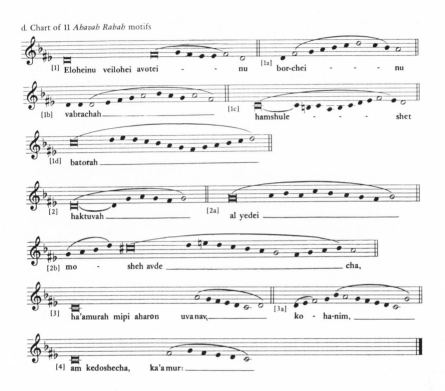

EXAMPLE 5.12, *continued.*

Note how Salomon Sulzer's Example 5.12a, in syllabic density, seems less free than Gershon Ephros' Example 5.12b, in neumatic density. Both of these are more tightly structured than Berele Chagy's Example 5.12c, in melismatic density. All three realizations of the Priestly Bless- ing are equally valid, but a service chanted exclusively along any one of these lines would soon pale. Ideally, the three chant-styles constantly in- termesh. The three Principal Prayer modes do likewise, adding to the mix three Secondary Prayer modes, plus "authentic" and "plagal" forms of every mode, as the ensuing chapter explains.

Defining The Three Principal Prayer Modes:
Bibliography & Notes

1. WEISGAL, Adolph J: *Shirei Hayyim Ve-emunah*, Baltimore, published by the author (1950), page 16.
2. PINCHIK, Pierre: *The Repertoire of Hazzan Pinchik*, New York, Cantors Assembly (1964), pages 78–88.
3. SINGER, Josef: "Die Tonarten des traditionellen Synagogengesanges" (1866), *Sammlung Kantoralwissenschaftlischer Aufsaetze*, edited by Aron Friedmann, Berlin, Boas (1922), pages 90–100.
4. KAISER, Alois, and William Sparger: *Principal Melodies of the Synagogue*, Chicago, Rubovitz (1893), Preface, calling three scales, all on C̲, Synagogue "modes."
5. COHEN, Francis Lyon: "Music, Synagogal," *Jewish Encyclopedia*, London, Funk & Wagnalls (1905), Volume 9:120.
6. AVENARY, Hanoch: *The Concept of Mode in European Synagogue Chant*, Jerusalem, Yuval (1971), Volume 2:12.
7. HARRIS, Hyman H.: *Hebrew Liturgical Music*, New York, Shulsinger, (1950), page 25.
8. SENDREY, Alfred: *Music in Ancient Israel*, New York, Philosophical (1969), page 208.
9 HEILMAN, Samuel: *Synagogue Life*, Chicago, University of Chicago (1976), page 213.
10. AVENARY, Hanoch: "Shtayger," *Encyclopedia Judaica*, Jerusalem, Keter (1972), Volume 14:1464.
11 WEINTRAUB, Hirsch: *Schire Beth Adonai* (1859), Second edition, Leipzig, Kaufmann (1901), Foreword. Prayer chants resembling three of the eight original Church modes: Dorian (mistakenly named Aeolian); Mixolydian; and Phrygian, are classified *uralt* ('very old'). Prayer chants resembling the more recent Ionian mode are designated *alt* ('old').
12. SACHS, Curt: *The Rise of Music in the Ancient World, East and West*, New York, Norton (1943), page 285.
13. SPECTOR, Johanna L.: "Musical Tradition and Innovation," *Central Asia*, edited by Edward Allworth, New York, Columbia University (1967), pages 465; 477.
14. SENDREY (see item 8), page 215.
15. PLEASANTS, Henry: *The Great American Popular Singers*, New York, Simon & Schuster (1974), page 108.
16. IDELSOHN, Abraham Zvi: *Jewish Music*, New York, Holt (1929), page 73.
17. IDELSOHN, Abraham Zvi: "Songs of the Babylonian Jews," *Thesaurus of Hebrew Oriental Melodies*, Berlin, Hartz (1923), Volume II, pages 7–8.

18. IDELSOHN, Abraham Zvi: *Toledot Haneginah Ha'ivrit*, Tel Aviv, Dvir (1924), page 21.
19. IDELSOHN (see item 18), pages 118–141; see **CHAPTER FOUR, The Many Faces Of Neume Motifs**, note 31, for the 16 Diaspora traditions analyzed.
20. ROSOWSKY, Solomon: *Neume Motifs for the Yearly Cycle of Biblical Chant According to the Lithuanian Tradition*, after manuscripts, New York, Jewish Theological Seminary (1958); Appendix B, line IV RES, neume groups 1. and 2.
21. IDELSOHN (see item 18), page 141.
22. IDELSOHN, Abraham Zvi: "The Traditional Songs of the South German Jews," *Thesaurus of Hebrew Oriental Melodies*, Leipzig, Hofmeister (1932), Vol. VII, page xx.
23. POWERS, Harold S.: "Mode," *The New Grove Dictionary of Music and Musicians*, edited by Stanley Sadie, London, MacMillan (1980), Volume 12:423.
24. WERNER, Eric: *The Sacred Bridge*, New York, Columbia University (1959); page 469.
25. IDELSOHN (see item 22), page xx; "The Synagogue Songs of the East European Jews," *Thesaurus of Hebrew Oriental Melodies*, Leipzig, Hofmeister (1933), Volume VIII, number 32.
26. LOEWE, Herbert: *Medieval Hebrew Minstrelsy*, London, James Clark (1926), page 80.
27. RABINOWITZ, H.: "Musaf Kedushah," *Sabbath Kit*, edited by Max Wohlberg, New York, Jewish Theological Seminary (circa 1950).
28. SCHNIPELISKY, Elias: "The Marriage Service," *The Best Cantorial Works of Cantor Mordechai Hershman*, Volume I, recording, New York, Greater Recording Company (1973), GRC 52, side A, band 1; transcribed by Joseph A. Levine.
29. IDELSOHN (see item 18), pages 14–17.
30. HAF traditions: [Lith] (see item 20, line II); [Bab] (see item 18, page 193, line 1); [Ash] (see item 18, page 193, line 9).
31. BAER, Abraham: *Baal T'fillah*, Gothenburg, published by the author (1877), number 409.
32. VINAVER, Chemjo: *Anthology of Jewish Music*, New York, Marks (1955), pages 221–222.
33. KALECHNIK, Abraham: *Zluso D'abraham*, Kishinev, published by the author (circa 1900), page 27.
34. SHLISKY, Joseph: *And on the Sabbath*, recording, New York, Collectors Guild (1960), CG 601, side 1, band 4; transcribed by Joseph A. Levine.
35. WERNER, Eric: *A Voice Still Heard*, University Park, Pennsylvania State University (1976), page 50.
36. IDELSOHN (see item 16), pages 28–30.
37. IDELSOHN (see item 17), number 212.
38. IDELSOHN (see item 16), page 11.

39. IDELSOHN (see item 22), page xxiv.
40. BERMAN, Edward: *Middle Eastern Roots of East European Chazanut*, New York, Jewish Theological Seminary (1979), page 12.
41. WERNER (see item 35), page 53; *Ahavah Rabah* governs 85 percent of Chasidic song repertories.
42. SAMINSKY, Lazare: *Music of the Ghetto and the Bible*, New York, Bloch (1932), page 68; WERNER (see item 35), page 57.
43. GLANTZ, Leib: "The Musical Basis of Nusach Hatefillah," New York, *Cantors Assembly Proceedings* (1952), 5:21.
44. NETTL, Bruno: "Folk and Traditional Music of the Western Continents," *History of Music Series*, edited by H. Wiley Hitchcock, Englewood Cliffs, Prentice-Hall, Second edition (1973), pages 84–85.
45. IDELSOHN (see item 25: 1933), number 232.
46. COHEN, Francis Lyon: "Cantillation," *Jewish Encyclopedia*, London, Funk & Wagnalls (1903), Volume 3:538.
47. SULZER, Salomon: *Schir Zion* (Vienna, 1839–1865), revised by Joseph Sulzer, Vienna (1905), number 91.
48. EPHROS, Gershon: "Shabbat," *Cantorial Anthology*, New York, Bloch (1953), Volume IV, page 237.
49. CHAGY, Berele: *Sweet Singer of Israel*, Volume II, recording, New York, Greater Recording Company (1973), GRC 34, side 1, band 4; transcribed by Joseph A. Levine.

CHAPTER SIX

MODAL INTERCHANGE:

Two Secondary Modes; "Authentic" and"Plagal" Forms of Every Mode; The Three-Part Selichah Mode

In this chapter we will clarify the manner in which Prayer modes interchange. Frequently, the three Principal ones interchange among themselves, with two Secondary modes (Ukranian-Dorian—a Slavic variation in minor, and Study—leaping octaves, fifths, fourths, and thirds), and with Selichah (a three-part 'Forgiveness' sequence). There are further interchanges of "authentic" with "plagal" forms of every mode. Contemporary American Synagogue practice has stressed the "plagal" middle section of the three-part Selichah mode, known as *Techinah* ('Pleading').

Liturgical Breathing-Space

Within each Prayer mode, changing intervals and tonal centers create endless variation. Cantors pride themselves on their ability to glide from one mode to another without changing stride. Their characteristic chant is a blend of disparate modalities, whether intentionally or otherwise, into a cohesive whole. Musical ideas flow from the prayer-texts, shifting to accommodate liturgical mood-changes. In certain portions of each service the chant seems to straddle several modes at once, taking on nuances that tie it to other liturgical moments. This is the breathing-space of Jewish worship, programmed, in Steven Lorch's words, "so that the ambiguities . . . of the music may be taken in before one is pushed into new sections and their multiple meanings."[1]

Prayer-mode mixing frees cantor and congregation from the tyranny of an all-too-familiar liturgy. We may take for example the essence of Rosh Hashanah Musaf: *Malchuyot* ('Kingship' verses); *Zichronot* ('Remembrance' verses); and *Shofarot* ('Revelation' verses). Convention dictates that *Malchuyot* be sung in *Adonai Malach, Zichronot* in *Magein Avot,* and *Shofarot* again in *Adonai Malach.* Yet the most celebrated practitioner during America's "superstar-cantor era, 1912–1916," Yossele Rosenblatt (1882–1933), sang *Teka,* the conclusion of *Shofarot,* in a mixed mode (EXAMPLE 6.1).[2]

Eloheinu veilohei avoteinu, teka . . .
'Our and God of our forbears,
sound the great Shofar for our freedom,
raise the signal to ingather our exiles . . .
[as prescribed] through thy servant Moses . . .
For thou hearest the sound of the Shofar'.

EXAMPLE 6.1
Mixed mode in Rosh Hashanah Musaf.

The first six measures are in *Magein Avot*. Measures seven and eight move to *Adonai Malach*; measure nine returns to *Magein Avot*. Measures ten through fourteen revisit *Adonai Malach*, until a final commitment to the original mode, *Magein Avot*, at measure fifteen. (Double-bar lines [I I] signal the mode changes; double-diagonal lines [/ /] indicate skips in the music).

Modally mixed Example 6.1 represents the breathing-space of Rosh Hashanah Musaf, when a congregation's temporal awareness is mythic rather than historical. Historian Yosef Yerushalmi elaborates:

> The present historical moment possesses little independent value . . . through the recitation of a myth, historical time is . . . shattered and one can experience again, if only briefly, the true time of origins and archetypes.[3]

Shofarot tells the central myth of Judaism—God's revelation at Sinai—in the Laudatory mode, *Adonai Malach*. Still, Rosh Hashanah is the Day of Judgement, traditionally when humankind's fate is decided for the coming year. So cantors invoke *Magein Avot*—the Didactic mode—a musical reminder of God's promise to Abraham, even as they praise Him. Worshippers thus enter the realm of mythic time; Mount Sinai (site of God's revelation to Moses) and Mount Moriah (site of God's promise to Abraham) merge in the congregation's collective subconscious, even though the great Shofar of Freedom is yet to be sounded.

During Shabbat Musaf, the seventh part of Kedushah provides similar breathing-space.

Echad hu eloheinu . . .
'One is our God, our Father, our Saviour; and
He in his mercy will again proclaim to us, in
the presence of all living, that He is our God'.

Salomon Sulzer seems to interpret this passage in a mode that is either *Adonai Malach* or *Ahavah Rabah*; parenthesized accidentals in EXAMPLE 6.2a[4] offer a solution to the puzzle. This transcription was published by Sulzer's son, Joseph, in 1905, fifteen years after Salomon's death and some fifty years after the piece's performance. The original 1839 edition had no music for the text, merely the instruction, *in ausdrucksvoller Weise* ('in an expressive way'); cantors should improvise the passage. Judging from contemporary reports of the Vienna *Ritus* as

EXAMPLE 6.2

Sulzer's modal interchange (*Adonai Malach* without parenthesized accidentals/*Ahavah Rabah* using parenthesized accidentals).

well as from the general modal scheme of Sulzer's Sabbath Morning service, this was its quintessential moment.

Sulzer consistently alternates *Adonai Malach* with *Ahavah Rabah* in the 1839 edition, so why not in the 1905 Kedushah? Since the surrounding paragraphs are set in *Adonai Malach*, the music of Example 6.2a would logically be in *Ahavah Rabah*, the mode Idelsohn characterizes as "full of fire and romanticism . . . of pain, of love, and faith in God."[5] The sharpened F̲ in new motif [2b] (compare with Example 5.12d)—creating an additional augmented-second interval between the mode's sixth and seventh degrees—increases the 'pain'. The altered *Ahavah Rabah* mode of Example 6.2a corresponds to the Arabic *Makam Hijaz-kar* of EX- AMPLE 6.2b,[6] and also to one of the two Secondary Prayer modes, Ukranian-Dorian, defined below (see Examples 6.3 through 6.5, and especially Example 6.4).

Sulzer's shift from *Adonai Malach* to *Ahavah Rabah* in Kedushah accompanies the text's transition from praise ('Holy, holy, holy') to petition ('in mercy again proclaim').

To feel the vocal difference, sing the first line-and-a half of Example 6.2a omitting the parenthesized accidentals. After that, observe all accidentals, parenthesized or not. Listeners, anticipating a continuation of the *Adonai Malach* mood of extolment, will be emotionally quickened by the sudden switch to supplication in the middle of line 2 (*Adonai Malach* motif [1b] with a flatted sixth degree, E̲♭).

An alert congregation cannot but savor the cantor's modal allusion to redemption at *berachamav* ('He in his mercy'). The reference is not only to time—the Messianic Age—but to place: Jerusalem. Sulzer uses the same sequence of rising *Ahavah Rabah* motifs—featuring 'painful' *Hijaz-kar* motif [2b]—in the Rosh Hashanah Musaf prayer, *Vete'erav*.

Hasheiv shechinatcha letsiyon . . .
'Restore thy presence to Zion, and the
Priestly rite to Jerusalem' (EXAMPLE 6.2c).[7]

He repeats almost the identical pattern in the Yom Kippur Neilah Atonement prayer: *Adonai, adonai . . .* ('The Lord . . . is merciful . . . forgive our iniquity'). The passage, EXAMPLE 6.2d,[8] is in *Ahavah Rabah*, but Sulzer sets the stage with *Adonai Malach*, twice quoting *Barechu*-type *Misinai* Tune ③ .

Any passage can serve as the breathing-space of a particular service, to imply redemption, ingathering, forgiveness, etc., through calculated blending of the three Principal Prayer modes. Here we have seen how High Holy Day awe permeates Sulzer's Shabbat Kedushah, forging a mood of both this world and the next. Worshippers absorb all of these nuances subliminally; the cantor's multi-faceted song glints with seasonal allusions before ushering in a new section with its own series of liturgical overtones.

Secondary Modes

The Ukranian-Dorian Mode

EXAMPLE 6.3[9] shows a musically more adventuresome realization of the *Adonai Malach* mode. In typically Eastern Ashkenazic fashion, it concludes Psalm 96, one of five Psalms added as Friday Night prelude to Psalm 93, by 16th-century Kabbalist mystics living in the Galilee town of Safed.

> *Yismechu hashamayim vetageil*
> *ha'arets . . .*
> 11. 'Let the heavens be glad, and let the earth rejoice; let the sea roar, and all that fills it;
> 12. let the field exult, and everything in it! Then shall the trees of the wood sing for joy
> 13. before the Lord, for he comes, for he comes to judge the earth. He will judge the world with righteousness, and the peoples with his truth'.

Example 6.3 alters the normal *Adonai Malach* intervals (D–E–F♯–G–A–B–C–D) by substituting F♮ for F♯, and G♯ for G. The accidentals F♮ and G♯ transform *Adonai Malach* into Ukranian-Dorian, a secular mode drawn from Gentile Balkan folk song. Its introduction imparts a Slavic-Oriental flavor, and illustrates a special kind of Prayer-mode fluidity: skilled cantors can change one mode into another by inserting or removing accidentals within melismatic runs. Example 6.3 introduces Ukranian-Dorian (verse 13., motif [2b]) in a run that encompasses 10 notes. It returns to *Adonai Malach* in motif [1c] via a run encompassing three notes. Some would describe the introduction of Ukranian-Dorian as modal coloring rather than modal mixing, since this Secondary 'mode' exists only as a motif within other Prayer modes. However, it may stand alone in secular song, as we observe next.

EXAMPLE 6.3
Adonai Malach mode with Ukranian-Dorian motif.

Ukranian-Dorian—as its name implies—occurs in Jewish folk song of Eastern Europe, but only rarely.[10] Yet it figures prominently in Modal technique. Along with a minor third, it features raised fourth-and-sixth degrees, which give its quintessential motif, [2b], a feeling of yearning. We see this in a Yiddish love song:

> *Di Mame Hot Mir Geshikt . . .*
> 'When Mother sent me to buy a box, the
> young sales clerk fell in love with me'
> (EXAMPLE 6.4).[11]

Notice how the ends of the first three lines rise in the love song. But in Example 6.3 (Psalm 96), the one Ukranian-Dorian motif ([2b]) acts as counterweight to an ascending *Adonai Malach* motif (verse 13., motif [2]) by *descending*. The folk element, Ukranian-Dorian of Example 6.4, has been subtly altered during its absorption into Synagogue song (Example 6.3).

EXAMPLE 6.4
A Yiddish love song in Ukranian-Dorian mode.

Ukranian-Dorian colors *Magein Avot* passages as well; two settings by the cantor of Rostow-on-Don, Eliezer Gerovitch (1844–1914), demonstrate. EXAMPLE 6.5a[12] sets the fifth strophe of the Shabbat Shacharit Piyyut, *Eil Adon* ('God, The Lord Over All Creation').

> *Pe'eir vechavod notenim lishmo . . .*
> 'Glory and honor they give to his name; and
> joyously sing of his unending fame. He
> fashioned the sun, and it shone forth in light;
> he called on the moon to illumine the night'.

Ukranian-Dorian again enters as motif [2b] of the modal sequence (end of line 2 and beginning of line 3, Example 6.5a), but in *Magein Avot* it is based on the third degree (F), rather than on the tonic (D), as in *Adonai Malach* (Example 6.3).

Lines between the opening and closing parentheses of EXAMPLE 6.5b,[13] are the prayer, *Eloheinu . . . Retseh* (same text as Friday Night *Magein Avot* Examples 5.9a–c, but here sung in *Ahavah Rabah* as part of the Sabbath Morning Amidah).

> Our God and God of our forbears, accept our
> rest; hallow us through thy commandments
> and grant our portion in thy law . . .
> Purify our hearts to serve thee in truth.

The two sections in parentheses of Example 6.5b precede and follow *Eloheinu . . . Retseh* in Gerovitch's collection, rounding out the *Ahavah Rabah* mode with motifs [1b] and [1].

Yimloch adonai le'olam . . .

'The Lord will reign for ever, thy God, O Zion,
to all generations. Praise the Lord'!
(Psalm 146:10);

Yevarechecha adonai veyishmerecha

'The Lord bless you and keep you'
(Numbers 6:24).

EXAMPLE 6.5
Ukranian-Dorian motif in *Magein Avot* and *Ahavah Rabah* passages.

Retseh opens with motif [4], one whole step below the tonic, D, and emphasizes [2], [2a], and [2b], all centering around the fourth degree, G. This loosens the tonic's pull, allowing the chant to 'float' its languid, neume-like melismas. Motif [2b] adds a double dash of exoticism to *Ahavah Rabah*: a) by raising C and E it introduces Ukranian-Dorian; and b) by raising C it makes the altered mode correspond to Arabic *Makam Hijaz-kar* (see Example 6.2b, pitched a fourth higher, on G). Note that Ukranian-Dorian within the *Ahavah Rabah* mode builds upon the *fourth* degree (G) rather than upon the *third* degree (F), as in *Magein Avot*, or than upon the *tonic* (D), as in *Adonai Malach*.

The Study Mode

The so-called Study mode is more a series of chordal outlines imposed on any of the three Principal Prayer modes than a complete mode. It got its name from the way in which Eastern European Jews studied the Talmud, leaping octaves and pausing on the intervening chordal degrees, as they formulated their arguments. Chords may be outlined in several ways: descending from third to tonic and ascending to the fifth ([3–1–5]); overtaking the tonic from below ([₁5–3–1]); rising through the tonic triad ([1–3–5]); descending from upper to lower tonic ([1^1–5–1]); etc. The [1^1–5–1] formula repeated—with pauses on the intervening chordal degrees (bold), making it [5–1^1–5–**6**–**4**–5] [1–**4**–1^1–5–1]—occurs as a two-part *Adonai Malach* phrase in the children's Four Questions, posed during the Passover Eve Haggadah ('telling') of the Israelites' Exodus from Egypt (EXAMPLE 6.6a).[14]

> *Shebechol haleilot anu ochlin . . .*
> 'On all other nights we may eat either
> leavened or unleavened bread, but on this
> night, only unleavened bread'.

The formula also occurs in *Magein Avot*, while studying either a Mishnah or Baraita (statements of law constituting the oldest parts of the Talmud), as in the final paragraph of the Babylonian Talmud's treatise, Berachot ('Blessings', EXAMPLE 6.6b).[15]

> *Amar rabi elazar . . .*
> 'Rabbi Elazar said in the name of Rabbi
> Chanina:
> "Scholars increase peace throughout the
> world" '.

The $[1^1\text{–}5\text{–}1]$ formula sometimes occurs in *Ahavah Rabah*, when the Gemara (general-discussion portion of the Talmud) is being studied, as in the case of two claimants to the same object: Babylonian Talmud, treatise Baba Metsia ('Middle Gate') 3b; EXAMPLE 6.6c.[16]

> *Vehoda'at ba'al din . .*
> 'A claimant's admission equals the testimony
> of 100 witnesses;
> "money" here means "fine" '.

To show the Study mode's consistency, switch the modes of all three examples, i.e., sing *Adonai Malach* Example 6.6a to *Ahavah Rabah* intervals (lower the sixth degree to B♭), sing *Magein Avot* Example 6.6b to *Adonai Malach* intervals (raise the third degree to F♯), sing *Ahavah Rabah* Example 6.6c to *Adonai Malach* intervals (lower the third degree to F♮ while raising the second degree to E♮), and so on.

Notice how the effect hardly differs no matter what the Prayer mode. That is because tonal figurations overpower pitch differences. Motifs, in other words, generally dominate modal intervals.

a. *Adonai Malach* (Passover Eve Haggadah); *Ahavah Rabah* intervals in parentheses)

Sheb-chol haleilot anu   ochelin chameits umatsah,   ha-lailah   ha-zeh kulo   matsah.

b. *Magein Avot* (Baraita, Treatise Berachot; *Adonai Malach* intervals in parentheses)

Amar rabi elazar, amar rabi chanina: Talmidei chachamim   marbim shalom ba-o   lam;

c. *Ahavah Rabah* (Gemara, Treatise Baba Metsi'a; *Magein Avot* intervals in parentheses)

Vehoda'at   ba'al din kemei'ah   eidim   da - mi;   meima-mon ke-nas.

EXAMPLE 6.6
Study mode cuts across the three Principal Prayer modes.

EXAMPLE 6.7

The Study mode in *Magein Avot* passages.

EXAMPLE 6.7a[17] illustrates five Study-mode tonic-triad inversions in *Magein Avot*: [3–1–5]; [₁5–1–3]; [1–5–3]; [1–3–₁5]; and [₁5–1–3]. The text is from a Mishnah: Peah ('Gleanings') 1.1; recited in the early-morning Preliminary service, *Birkot Hashachar.*

Eilu devarim she'ein lahem shi'ur . . .
'These are the things for which no measure is
prescribed:
leaving the corner of one's field for the poor;
the First-fruit offering;
the Festal offering; deeds of lovingkindness;
and the study of Torah'.

EXAMPLE 6.7b adds four combinations of leaping fourths, thirds, octaves, and fifths: [₁5–1–4]; [1–4–1]; [1¹–1]; and [1–3–5–1¹–5].

EXAMPLE 6.7c[18] shows six more motifs, along with their Lithuanian neume-motif equivalents: [4–1–3]; [1–5–4]; [5–4–5–3]; [3–4]; [4–1¹–1]; and [3–2–3–4–1] (compare the Parallels with same references in Appendix B). These motifs appear as part of the *Magein Avot*-mode when study—as opposed to prayer—is called for. They are either direct quotes, extensions, or variations of *Magein Avot* mode motifs charted in Example 5.9d, and bear corresponding bracketed phrase-numbers alongside their neume-motif references. The Biblical text is God's exhortation that the Israelites remember His words, so that their days and their children's days will be multiplied.

al ha'adamah asher nishba . . .
'in the land which the Lord swore to your
fathers to give them, as long as the heavens
are above the earth'
(Deuteronomy 11:21).

"Authentic" and "Plagal" Forms of Every Mode

There remains to explain another fundamental method of modal interchange, namely between the "authentic" and "plagal" forms of every mode. The *Harvard Dictionary of Music* places the characteristic range of an "authentic" mode from its final note to an octave above, and that of a "plagal" mode from a fourth below its final note to a fifth above (1972:165). This definition has nothing to do with major or minor but rather with the concentration of melodic activity in relation to the tonic. EXAMPLE 6.8 offers an "authentic" and a "plagal" version of the Night-prayer, *Hashkiveinu*:

Hashkiveinu, adonai eloheinu, leshalom . . .

'Cause us, O God, to lie down in peace, and raise
us up, O our king, to life. Spread over us thy
tabernacle of peace; direct us aright through thy
good counsel; save us for thy name's sake.
Shield us from enemy, pestilence, sword,
famine, and sorrow. Remove the adversary surrounding us, shelter us beneath thy wings'.

EXAMPLE 6.8a,[19] by Adolph Katchko, moves from "authentic"
Ahavah Rabah (lines 1–3+) to "authentic" *Magein Avot* (lines 3+–6). In
both modes, the motifs move generally between the tonic (F in the opening *Ahavah Rabah*; Bb in the continuing *Magein Avot*) and almost an
octave above. As before, double-bar lines (❘❘) mark each modal change.

EXAMPLE 6.8b,[20] by Jacob Bachmann, moves from "plagal" *Adonai
Malach* (lines 1–3) to the "plagal" harmonic-minor mode featured in the
middle section of the three-part Selichah mode (lines 4–5), examined in
more detail shortly. Note that the harmonic-minor mode of Selichah uses
a leading tone—or half step—between its seventh degree (raised from Bb
to B♮) and tonic (C). An "authentic" *Ahavah Rabah* transition (lines 6–7)
carries the piece to a "plagal" *Adonai Malach* ending (end of line 7, and
line 8). The opening and closing *Adonai Malach* sections are "plagal" because the motifs move generally between a fourth below the *Adonai
Malach* tonic, Bb, and a fifth above. Similarly, the section we called harmonic-minor is "plagal" because the motifs move generally between a
fourth below its tonic, C, and a fifth above. The *Ahavah Rabah* transi-
tion-section is "authentic" because the motifs move generally between
the *Ahavah Rabah* tonic, F, and an octave above.

All the Principal Prayer-mode Examples cited so far (Examples 5.3–
5.12) are "authentic." The composite charts, however, include "Plagal"
motifs: [1d], [1e], [1f], [2], and [2a] for *Adonai Malach* in Example 5.6d;
[2], [3a], [3c], [4], and [4b] for *Magein Avot* in Example 5.9d; [1c], [1d],
[2b], [3], and [4] for *Ahavah Rabah* in Example 5.12d.

Roughly two-thirds (29) of the Principal Prayer-mode motifs are
"authentic," and one-third (15), "plagal." A like proportion holds for
Biblical neume motifs (185:63; as charted in Appendix B). The proportion differs for the *Misinai* Tunes charted in Appendix C; over half (20)
are "plagal." The greater proportion of "plagal" *Misinai* Tunes explains
why so many appear in the "plagal" harmonic-minor section of the three-
part Selichah mode (Example 6.8b, lines 4–5), which we now examine.

EXAMPLE 6.8
"Authentic" and "Plagal" *Hashkiveinu*-settings.

The Three–part Selichah Mode

The Selichah ('Forgiveness') mode, dating from Second-temple days, chooses from among three different modes in each of its three sections:

> Section 1—*Vidui* ('Confessional'), uses either "authentic"
> *Adonai Malach* or "authentic" *Magein Avot*;
> Section 2—*Techinah* ('Pleading'), uses "plagal" harmonic-minor
> (refer to lines 4–5 of Example 6.8b);
> Section 3—*Nechamah* ('Consolation'), uses either "authentic"
> *Adonai Malach* or "authentic" *Magein Avot*
> (like Section 1—*Vidui*).

EXAMPLE 6.9a[21] shows a *Vidui*-section—whose text is Biblical—set in *Adonai Malach.*

> *Selach na la'avon ha'am hazeh . . .*
> 'Pardon the iniquity of this people according
> to the greatness of thy mercy'
> (Numbers 14:19).

EXAMPLE 6.9b[22] illustrates how a *Nechamah*-section—with Babylonian Talmud text—also set in *Adonai Malach*, resembles *Vidui*, with the order of its *Misinai* Tunes reversed.

> *Tsadikim anachnu . . .*
> 'We are righteous . . .yet indeed we have
> sinned' (Yoma ['Atonement'], 87b).

When comparing the *Misinai* Tunes cited in Example 6.9b with Appendix C, transpose the notes mentally to the same pitch level and look for the *essential* motif. Remember that every cantor realizes the musical idea differently.

Nechamah (and so *Vidui* as well) is sometimes sung to *Magein Avot*, using Study-mode chordal leaps, as EXAMPLE 6.9c[23] demonstrates. This text and the majority that follow are composed by *payyetanim* (liturgical poets), either as an individual verse (*Selichah*), or as grouped verses (*Sidrei Selichot*, Example 3.11: Category III, PENITENTIAL LAMENTS, Prayer-types –q– and –r–).

> *Chatanu, tsureinu . . .*
> 'We have sinned, O our God; forgive us, O our
> Creator' (Yom Kippur Musaf).

The *Nechamah*-section's *Magein Avot* mode is often colored by Ukranian-Dorian, as in EXAMPLE 6.9d.[24]

> *Vehasheiv shevut . . .*
> 'Restore the peaceful homes of Jacob, and
> deliver us for thy name's sake'
> (Yom Kippur Neilah).

Or the *Nechamah*-section's mode may be *Adonai Malach*, resolving into *Magein Avot*, as in EXAMPLE 6.9e.[25]

> *Ki vesheim kodshecha . . .*
> 'For in thy holy name we have trusted'
> (Yom Kippur Maariv).

EXAMPLE 6.9f[26] demonstrates how the Selichah mode's opening and closing sections are easily confused, since *Vidui* may also open in *Magein Avot* (compare with Example 6.9b).

> *Eil, melech yosheiv . . .*
> 'Almighty King, who sitteth on the
> Mercy-throne, thou dost act graciously'
> (Yom Kippur Maariv).

EXAMPLE 6.9
The Selichah mode's opening (*Vidui*) and closing (*Nechamah*) sections:
modal options are all "authentic."

e. *Nechamah* in *Adonai Malach/Magein Avot*

Ki   ve-sheim kod- she - cha _____ va - tach - nu,

f. *Vidui* in *Magein Avot*

Eil,   melech   yosheiv al kisei   racha - mim, mitna- heig-bacha-si - dut,

EXAMPLE 6.9, *continued.*

Whatever their Prayer mode, both *Vidui and Nechamah* are sung to "authentic" motifs. Not so the Selichah mode's middle, or *Techinah*-section, which is sung to "plagal" motifs exclusively. The Kol Nidre prayer is a *Techinah*-section par excellence. A thousand-year-old Aramaic legal declaration, Kol Nidre seeks forgiveness from 'all personal vows which we are likely to make between this Day of Atonement and the next'. Its initial motif (EXAMPLE 6.10a),[27] sets the "plagal" harmonic-minor pattern, moving between the tonic (B♭) and the fourth below, via a raised seventh degree (leading-tone, A♮).

> *Kol nidre ve'esarei . . .*
> 'Let all personal vows . . .[be null and void]'.

EXAMPLE 6.10b compares the *Techinah* motifs of Kol Nidre to lines 4–5 of Example 6.8b, the central portion of *Hashkiveinu*. The *Hashkiveinu*-text, beginning: *Vehagein Ba'adeinu* ('Shield us from enemy, pestilence, sword, famine, and sorrow'); is the second best-known *Techinah*, or 'Pleading'-section, in the liturgy, after Kol Nidre. This setting of *Vehagein Ba'adeinu*, by Jacob Bachmann (1846–1905), paraphrases the *Techinah* motifs of Kol Nidre. The tonic for both Prayer-mode chants is B♭. Motifs move generally between the fourth below to the fifth above, using the raised-seventh degree, A♮, as the leading-tone. Because Kol Nidre is the mother lode of *Misinai* Tunes as well as the classic *Techinah*-section, its motifs bear *Misinai* numbers in squares (☐), keyed to Appendix C.

a. Initial motif of Kol Nidre

b. Outline of Selichah mode's *Techinah*-section

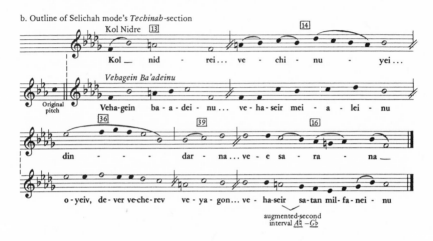

EXAMPLE 6.10
Comparison of two middle (*Techinah*)-sections of a Selichah mode: Kol Nidre; and *Vehagein Ba'adeinu* (from *Hashkiveinu*).

Kol Nidre represents Prayer-type III.r in Example 3.11—PENITENTIAL LAMENTS (*Selichot*)—and in Appendix C—'Grouped Composed Verses' (*Sidrei Pesukim*). Sung as the middle (*Techinah*)-section of the three-part Selichah mode, it is surrounded by a *Vidui* ('Confessional') opening and a *Nechamah* ('Consolation') closing. EXAMPLE 6.11a[28] shows the Selichah mode's *Vidui*-section in "authentic" *Magein Avot*, as opening Confessional to Kol Nidre. (*Misinai Tunes* 34 , 33 , 16 and 31 are numbered in squares).

Bishivah shel ma'alah . . .

'By authority of the Court on high and by authority of the Court below, with heavenly consent and with the consent of this congregation, we declare it permissible to pray together with the sinners'.

EXAMPLE 6.11b[29] shows the Selichah mode's *Nechamah*-section in "authentic" *Adonai Malach*, as closing Consolation to Kol Nidre, (*Misinai* Tunes 1 , 2 , and 4 are numbered in squares).

Venislach lechol adat . . .

'And the congregation of the people of Israel shall be forgiven, and the stranger who sojourns among them, because the whole population was involved in the error' (Numbers 15:26).

a. "Authentic" opening in *Magein Avot*

Original pitch — Bishivah shel ma'alah uvishivah shel ma-tah, al da'at hamakom ve'al da'at hakahal, anu matirin lehitpaleil im ha'avarya-nim.

b. "Authentic" closing in *Adonai Malach*

Ve-nis-lach le-chol a-dat be-nei yis-ra-eil vela-geir ha-gar be-to-cham ki lechol ha'am bishga-gah.

EXAMPLE 6.11

Opening *Vidui* (Confessional) and closing *Nechamah* (Consolation) of a Selichah mode whose middle-section *Techinah* (Plea) is Kol Nidre.

Interchange Between the Selichah and *Ahavah Rabah* Modes

The Selichah mode's prime source of interchange—as has been noted—is that of *Vidui* with *Nechamah*. In addition, the *Techinah*-section's raised-seventh degree (A♮, assuming B♭ as tonic, as in Example 6.10) creates an augmented-second interval (A♮–G♭; see the final motif in Example 6.10, lower staff, marked by a **V**). The "plagal" harmonic-minor motifs moving between the fifth degree (F) and the tonic (B♭)—using this augmented-second interval—also belong to an "authentic" *Ahavah Rabah* mode built upon F.

The legendary 18th-century cantor, Salomon Weintraub (1781–1829), constantly alternated a Selichah mode's *Techinah*-section—which we shall henceforth designate Selichah-*Techinah*—with *Ahavah Rabah*.

a. "Authentic" *Ahavah Rabah* on F̲ / "Plagal" Selichah-*Techinah* on B̲♭

EXAMPLE 6.12
Weintraub's modal interchange on Shabbat-Rosh Chodesh:
alternating "authentic" and "plagal" forms of *Ahavah Rabah* and
Selichah-*Techinah* modes.

EXAMPLE 6.12a[30] is from the Shabbat Musaf Amidah when it coincides with the New Moon (Rosh Chodesh).

> *Atah yatsarta olamcha mikedem . . .*
> 'Thou didst form thy world from of old . . .
> thou hast loved and favored us, raised us up
> and called us by thy holy name'.

Notice how the chant vacillates between "authentic" *Ahavah Rabah* on F (bracketed motifs [1a], [1b]) and "plagal" Selichah-*Techinah* on B♭ (boxed *Misinai* Tunes 14 , 36 , 39 , 28 , 16). Double-bar lines (l l) mark modal changes, and a **V** underscores the augmented-second interval, A♮–G♭, common to both modes. Weintraub alternates *Ahavah Rabah* and Selichah-*Techinah* to prepare his listeners for the text's sudden shift from national pride to national mourning a few lines further (EXAMPLE 6.12b).

> *Ulefi shechatanu lefanecha . . .*
> 'But because we have sinned against thee,
> our city is destroyed, our Temple laid waste'.

The chant continues much as it began, vacillating between supplication (*Ahavah Rabah*) and pleading (Selichah-*Techinah*), enveloping the congregation in an intensely devotional mood consistent with the rarity of the occasion (Rosh Chodesh coincides with Shabbat only once or perhaps twice a year).

Authorities are divided on which Prayer mode shall prevail for this rare occasion. Solomon Rozumni, for instance, writes *Atah Yatsarta* in "authentic" *Magein Avot*.[31] Adolph Katchko begins similarly, but modulates to a "plagal" Selichah-*Techinah* on the fourth degree.[32] Alexander Ersler remains in "plagal" Selichah-*Techinah* throughout.[33] Yet a fourth authority, Abba Weisgal, begins in "authentic" *Ahavah Rabah* and modulates to "plagal" *Ahavah Rabah* on the fourth degree.[34]

As we have seen, Example 6.12b offers a fifth option. It vacillates between "authentic" *Ahavah Rabah* and "plagal" Selichah-*Techinah* before settling upon "plagal" *Ahavah Rabah* on the fourth degree.

The Selichah-*Techinah* motifs—*Misinai* Tunes 28 , 33 —and the *Ahavah Rabah* motifs—[3], [4]—in Example 6.12b are all "plagal" (compare their realization here with Appendix C and Example 5.12d; augmented-second intervals in "plagal" *Ahavah Rabah*—on B♭—are underscored in Example 6.12b by a **V** marking D–C♭).

Selichah-*Techinah* as a Fourth Principal Prayer Mode

The Selichah mode's *Techinah*-section (Selichah-*Techinah*) has become an independent Prayer mode in the United States, as we shall discover in the second chapter of **PART IV**. The next four musical Examples briefly show how American congregations use it throughout the year for: High Holy Day Amidah (EXAMPLE 6.13a);[35] Festival Amidah (EXAMPLE 6.13b);[36] Shabbat Amidah (EXAMPLE 6.13c);[37] and Friday Night Maariv (EXAMPLE 6.13d).[38]

> *6.13a—Veyomeru lecha chosecha . . .*
> 'Let those who trust in thee exclaim: "Be thou sanctified. O Lord, over all thy works"! '

> *6.13b—Avinu malkeinu, galeh . . .*
> 'Our Father, Our King . . . shine forth and be exalted . . . gather our dispersed from . . . the ends of the earth'.

> *6.13c—Baruch atah . . . hatov shimcha . . .*
> 'Blessed art thou, O Lord, whom it is fitting to praise'.

> *6.13d—Ki heim chayeinu . . .*
> 'For they are our life and the length of our days; we will meditate upon them day and night'.

The American Selichah-*Techinah* motifs have their origin in *Misinai* Tunes and so are cross-referenced with Appendix-C numeration. Yet there are differences. The upper staff of EXAMPLE 6.13e shows *Misinai* Tune [19], appearing in a Rosh Hashanah *Ofan* ('Concerning "Angels" ')-type Piyyut (see Example 3.11, II.h; and Appendix C, left-hand column):

> *Bochein kol eshtonot . . .*
> 'God discerns the thoughts of both low and high, this day'.

Note how the *Misinai* Tune is in a "plagal"-major *Adonai Malach* mode. *Misinai* Tune [19] changes to a "plagal" harmonic-minor Selichah-*Techinah* mode in its American version (Example 6.13e, lower staff, extension of Example 6.13a), a *Keva* passage from the cantor's repetition of the HHD Amidah for Musaf and Neilah.

[Tukdash, adon,] al kol ma'asecha . . .
'[Be sanctified, O Lord,] over all thy works'.

e. "Plagal"-major *Adonai-Malach Misinai* Tune 19 (upper staff), and its "plagal" harmonic-minor Selichah-*Techinah* American version

EXAMPLE 6.13
The Selichah-*Techinah* mode in American usage.

The parenthesized continuations on both staves reinforce their respective modalities: "plagal"-major *Adonai Malach* for the *Misinai* Tune; "plagal" harmonic-minor Selichah-*Techinah* for the American version. For whatever reasons, prevalence of the Selichah-*Techinah* mode in this country mirrors contemporary American Jewry's preference for prayer in "plagal" minor.

Is there something in the relationship of a mode's final note to the range of its motifs that sets it apart from other modes? At one time "authentic" modes were considered masculine, and "plagal" modes, feminine.[39] "Authentic" melodies, even when in minor, tend to sound stronger than their "plagal" counterparts, including those "plagal" counterparts written in major. The three Principal Prayer modes bear this out; while they include "plagal" motifs, they are predominantly "authentic" in character. *Adonai Malach* (major) sings praises; *Magein Avot* (minor) instructs; *Ahavah Rabah* (major, with minor second-and-sixth degrees) petitions. The two Secondary modes—Ukranian-Dorian and Study—are also predominantly "authentic." In short, they lead from strength. Only Selichah, the one mode begging pardon, features an exclusively "plagal" section. With its "authentic" opening and closing—both sometimes major, sometimes minor—it is the Prayer mode most susceptible to interchange as well.

EXAMPLE 6.14 combines 11 *Misinai* Tunes—all used with variations in Examples 6.10, 6.12, and 6.13—into a Selichah-*Techinah*-mode chart. Its text is the middle (*Techinah*)-section of *Hashkiveinu* (compare with Example 6.8b lines 4–5).

> *Vehagein ba'adeinu . . .*
> 'Shield us from enemy, pestilence, sword,
> famine, and sorrow. Remove the adversary
> surrounding us, shelter us beneath thy
> wings'.

Modes Carry Moods

Cantors traditionally tried to suit the atmosphere of each prayer to its liturgical moment. Particular modes were felt to work better at certain times of the year, month, week, or day. Each mode carried a characteristic mood, or *ethos,* after the ancient Greek doctrine set forth by Aristotle (*Metaphysics* 8.5). Medieval Jews believed that Prayer modes

EXAMPLE 6.14
Chart of the Selichah-*Techinah* mode, using 11 *Misinai* Tunes.

had the power to influence behavior. The *ethos* of Selichah led to contrition, of *Magein Avot* to learning, and of *Adonai Malach* to righteousness. British scholar David Wulstan traces the evolution of the Hebrew word for 'minstrel' (*menagein*, II Kings 3:15) from: to sing in a particular manner (*nagein*, Psalm 33:3); through 'taunt-song' (*manginah*, Lamentations 3:63); to 'enchantress' (*menageneh*, Ecclesiasticus 9:4).[40] Thus to medieval Jews each Prayer mode acted like a charm or enchantment.

To modern American Jews acquainted with the nuances of Synagogue song, prescribed motifs sung within modes at specific times conjure deep-seated feelings. The key to their effect lies in the history of musical associations that each worshipper brings to a service. An individual who has had no prior exposure to traditional chant will find Prayer modes all alike: hypnotically strange. Yet the musical language of *chazanut* perfectly suits traditional Jewish worship. It uses recognizable modes that fade one into another, sustaining the pervasive *ethos* through endless invention and age-old motivic allusion. It attunes a solo cantorial voice to the collective heartbeat of all assembled, with the result that, as in Solomon's Temple

'the song sings itself'.[41]

Modal Interchange: Two Secondary Modes; "Authentic" and "Plagal" Forms Of Every Mode; The Three-part Selichah Mode: Bibliography & Notes

1. LORCH, Steven Charles: *The Convergence of Jewish and Western Culture as Exemplified through Music*, New York, Columbia University (1977), page 141.
2. ROSENBLATT, Yossele: Tefiloth Josef, New York, Metro (1927), pages 38–39; ethnomusicologist Mark SLOBIN coined the term, "superstar-cantor era," (see item 10), pages 169–170.
3. YERUSHALMI, Yosef Hayim: *Zakhor*, Seattle, University of Washington (1982), pages 6–7.
4. SULZER, Salomon: *Schir Zion* (Vienna, 1839), revised by Joseph Sulzer, Vienna (1905), number 133.
5. IDELSOHN, Abraham Zvi: "The Traditional Song of the South German Jews," *Thesaurus of Hebrew Oriental Melodies*, Leipzig, Hofmeister (1932), Volume VII, page xxiv.
6. IDELSOHN, Abraham Zvi: *Toledot Haneginah Ha'ivrit*, Tel Aviv, Dvir (1924), page 27.
7. SULZER (see item 4), number 391.
8. SULZER (see item 4), number 457.
9. LEVINE, Joseph A.: *Emunat Abba* (Baltimore Hebrew College, 1981), Ann Arbor, University Microfilms, Volume II, number 255.
10. SLOBIN, Mark: *Tenement Songs*, Urbana, University of Illinois (1982), page 85. The Ukranian-Dorian mode occurs in 4.5% of Russo-Jewish folk songs and in 11% of Russo-Jewish dance tunes.
11. IDELSOHN (*Thesaurus*, see item 5), "The Folk Song of the East European Jews," Volume IX, number 594.
12. GEROVITCH, Eliezer: *Schirej Simroh*, Rostow-on-Don, published by the author (1904), page 32.
13. GEROVITCH (see item 12), pages 37–38.
14. BAER, Abraham: *Baal T'fillah*, Gothenburg, published by the author (1877), number 764.
15. ROSENBLATT, Yossele: *Ninety Minutes with Yossele Rosenblatt*, recording, New York, Shirim S–1001 (no date), side 3, band 6; transcribed by Joseph A. Levine.
16. IDELSOHN (*Thesaurus*, see item 5), "The Synagogue Song of the East European Jews," Volume VIII, number 234b.
17. RAPPAPORT, Jacob: "Eilu Devarim," in IDELSOHN (*Thesaurus*, see item 16), number 236.
18. SOORKIS, Moishele: "Lema'an Yirbu," *Cantorial Rarities*, recording, New York, Collectors Guild CG–609 (1961), side 2, band 2; transcribed by Joseph A. Levine.
19. KATCHKO, Adolph: *Hashkiveinu*, manuscript, New York, Hebrew Union College (circa 1950).

20. BACHMANN, Jacob: *Schirath Jacob*, Odessa, Jurgenson (1884), number 17.
21. FRIEDMANN, Aron: *Schir Lisch'laumau*, Berlin, Deutsche-Israelitischen Gemeindebunde (1901), number 398a.
22. HELLER, Josef: *Kol T'hilloh*, Brno, Winiker (1914), Volume II, number 260.
23. SULZER (see item 4), number 410b.
24. LEVINE (see item 9), Volume I, number 160c.
25. NAUMBOURG, Samuel: *Zemirot Yisraeil*, Paris, published by the author (1847), number 264b.
26. IDELSOHN (see item 6), page 282:a.
27. SCHORR, Baruch: *N'ginoth Baruch Schorr for New Year Day and Day of Atonement*, edited by Israel Schorr, New York, Bloch (1928), number 151.
28. LEVINE (see item 9), Volume I, number 84.
29. LEVINE (see item 9), Volume I, number 86.
30. WEINTRAUB, Hirsch: "Schire Schlomo" of Salomon Weintraub, Part III of *Schire Beth Adonai*, Koenigsberg, published by the author (1859), number 191.
31. ROZUMNI, Solomon: *Shirei Rozumni*, edited by Samuel Alman, London, Cailingold (1930), number 75.
32. KATCHKO, Adolph: *Thesaurus of Cantorial Liturgy*, New York, Hebrew Union College (1952), number 147.
33. ERSLER, Alexander: *T'hillah V'zimrah* (Wloclawek, 1907), reissued by Cantors Assembly, New York, (1958), number 53.
34. WEISGAL, Abba: (see LEVINE, item 9), Volume II, number 367.
35. SCHNIPELISKY, Eliyohu: *Nishmas Eliyohu*, New York, Metro (1949), number 69.
36. LEVINE (see item 9), Volume II, number 443.
37. KUSEVITSKY, David: *Cantorial Masterpieces,* recording, New York, Tikvah T–12 (circa 1957), side 1, band 1; transcribed by Joseph A. Levine.
38. EPHROS, Gershon: "Shabbat," *Cantorial Anthology,* New York, Bloch (1953), Volume IV, page 86.
39. POWERS, Harold S.: "Mode," *The New Grove Dictionary of Music and Musicians*, edited by Stanley Sadie, London, MacMillan (1980), Volume 12: 398–399.
40. WULSTAN, David: "The Origin of Modes," *Studies in Eastern Chant*, edited by Miloš Velimirović, London, Oxford (1971), Volume II, pages 7–8.
41. KIMCHI (see **PART I, JERUSALEM OF OLD**: note 1).

PART IV

PERFORMANCE TECHNIQUE

Jewish liturgy and ritual, so heavily charged with intricate associations to past and future . . . are like musical notations which, in themselves, cannot convey the nuances and textures of live performance.

Zakhor, 1982
Yosef Hayim Yerushalmi

CHAPTER SEVEN

Vocal Quality; Style; Improvisation; Prescribed Motifs

Performance technique, the fourth component of Synagogue song, is the most difficult to define, the only one of the four that cannot be exampled in print. Yet ways of employing the voice, styles of conducting a service, improvisation, and the creative use of prescribed motifs are far more important to conveying mood than written notes or words. In this chapter we explore three different vocal approaches: formal; emotional; and a blend of both. Readers have ample opportunity to try their hand at chants that commemorate major life-cycle events.

Vocal Quality

Determined by the liturgical occasion, each service must be sung in a particular way; vocal quality, dynamics, and phrasing are vital to establishing the right atmosphere. The words of Kaddish (EXAMPLE 7.1), for instance, sound different when sung at different times.

EXAMPLE 7.1
The words of Kaddish, sung at different times.

Yitgadal veyitkadash shemeh rabah . . .
'Magnified and sanctified be his great name
throughout the world which he hath created
according to his will. May he establish his
kingship in our lifetime'.

Changes of mode entail corresponding changes in the voice (which we cannot show). I urge the reader to make the discovery for him or herself by singing the six parts of Example 7.1 in succession. Running the gamut of Prayer modes discussed in **PART III**, the six parts occur on the occasions indicated, and should last the approximate amounts of time listed.

EXAMPLE 7.1a[1] —*Adonai Malach*—High Holy Day Maariv—
20 seconds.

EXAMPLE 7.1b[2] —*Magein Avot*—Festival Maariv—
35 seconds.

EXAMPLE 7.1c[3] —*Ahavah Rabah*—Shabbat Shacharit—
13 seconds.

EXAMPLE 7.1d[4] —Ukranian-Dorian—Friday Night Maariv—
20 seconds.

EXAMPLE 7.1e[5] —Study mode—Following Study session—
10 seconds.

EXAMPLE 7.1f[6] —Selichah-*Techinah*—Yom Kippur Neilah—
46 seconds.

Each example's duration, dynamic, and interpretative marking will help the reader in establishing a distinct mood, be it: exalted, contrite; peaceful; devout; solemn; etc. Aim for the mood, and vocal quality will follow. Introduce an occasional "speaking"-effect or *sprechgesang,* by dropping a motif-ending downward to an indefinite pitch (transcribed by a double-slur [⟩⟩], as in **PART II, CHAPTER TWO: Dramatizing Bible Chant**). Try it at *malchuteh,* the final word in each example.

Describing different vocal qualities is as subjective as producing them. No two voices sound alike, nor is a single voice heard alike by any two listeners. Moreover, no commonly accepted terminology exists in our culture to describe singing. The only word in English intended to quantify sound is "loud," whose opposite, "soft," borrows a tactile adjective. Other terms used to qualify sound are also borrowed: "rough" and "smooth" (tactile); "bright" and "dark" (visual); "nasal" and "throaty" (physiological); "hollow" and "full" (physical). Even a commonly used word such as "fine" falls short in describing voice, implying "superior" to some, "thin" to others.

Vocal quality also depends on its acoustical surroundings: contours of the room and type of amplification. Modern buildings generally use absorptive materials in construction, and do not allow sound to reverberate. Loudspeaker systems compensate only partly for this shortcoming, since they are engineered mostly for speech,[7] whose dynamic-and-frequency range is limited. Thus loudspeakers enhance the rabbinic readings which comprise much of American Jewish worship, but deter cantorial singing, which is loud and high-pitched.

In analyzing the shapes of buildings intended for musical performance, Michael Forsyth categorizes auditoriums as either "caves" or "open air."[8] For centuries, cantors had to overcome the cavernous echoes of large prayer halls by pushing their voices into a stridency no longer necessary. But habits persist. Today the more 'operatic' a cantor's singing, the more distorted it sounds when amplified.

Now, two generations after the so-called Golden Age of American *Chazanut*, with sound-deadened rooms neutralized by speech-oriented amplification, we have solved the "cave" problems described by Forsyth by recreating the "open air" conditions of antiquity. Levitical singers coped with non-reflective surroundings in the Temple courtyards by enunciating syllabically on single tones (we think), indulging their melismatic bent only after rhetorical points had been made. To flourish in an electronic age, cantorial phraseology must realign itself with its Levitical, Psalmodic-technique component. That is why this book transcribes much of its music, published originally in conventional notation, on reciting-tones. Seeing even familiar music notated Psalmodically induces a tonal solemnity and vocal flow that work well over a microphone. 'Whip-cracking' Example 1.2 confirms this; its declamation draws attention, and its cadenza delights the ear. Try recording it with amplification in an empty synagogue. Then listen again and again to the result, a vocal quality that seems to touch American Jews.

Style

In addition to vocal considerations, there are, historically, three approaches that determine the style of service in American synagogues. Samuel Vigoda, one of the last surviving Golden Age cantors, lists two:

Chazanut Haseider ('formal cantorial singing'); and *Chazanut Haregesh* ('emotional cantorial singing').[9] *Chazanut Haseider* offers a well-ordered ritual, polished but predictable. Original champions of this Apollonian approach, which flowered around the Black Sea port of Odessa over a century ago, included Bezalel Odesser (1790–1861) and Nisi Blumenthal (1805–1903). *Chazanut Haregesh*, the Dionysian or free-wheeling counterpart to Apollonian singing, thrived on intense emotional fervor. Centered in the Ukranian city of Berdichev, the chief proponents of this explosive style were Yeruchom Hakoton (1798–1891) and Nisi Belzer (1824–1906).

A third style, incorporating both Apollonian and Dionysian elements, grew from the practice of Salomon Sulzer. Called the Vienna *Ritus*, it was widely imitated. Elegant and highly organized, it often took wing in moments of fiery inspiration. The 'formal' and 'emotional' styles survive, respectively, in American Reform and Orthodox Judaism. The Vienna style is the ideal of Conservative Judaism, more in theory, however, than in practice.

Let's turn to a single prayer for comparing the three approaches, in both this and the previous century. Many earlier musical settings, unfortunately, are to texts no longer recited by all congregations. Conversely, some recent interpolations, such as the Prayer for the State of Israel, were unknown to prior generations. Happily, one prayer has persisted in the three branches of Judaism, throughout the 19th and 20th centuries, in both Europe and America: a High Holy Day Musaf meditation by Kalonymos ben Meshullam (11th century, Mayence, in the Rhineland). From that meditation, *Unetaneh Tokef* ('We Declare the Holiness of This Awesome Day'), we examine the passage depicting all living creatures passing before God for judgement.

> *Berosh hashanah yikateivun . . .*
> 'On Rosh Hashanah their fate is written, and
> on Yom Kippur their fate is sealed: how many
> shall leave the world and how many shall
> enter it; who shall live and who shall die'.

Kalonymos' meditation is technically a *Siluk-type* Piyyut ('Concerning "Heavenly ascent" '); mentioned as Category II.n in Example 3.11, and as *Misinai* Tune ⎯28⎯ in Appendix C.

In the absence of manuscripts for this prayer in all three styles, we must adapt musical settings bearing a similar *ethos* that were meant for other texts. Two such adapted settings are Nisi Blumenthal's *Shiviti* ('I keep the Lord always before me' [Psalm 16:8–9]; Yom Kippur Yizkor or Memorial Service), and Nisi Belzer's *Hayom* ('Today is the birthday of the world'; Rosh Hashanah Musaf). *Shiviti* (EXAMPLE 7.2a)[10] epitomizes the formal Odessa style of *Chazanut Haseider*, while *Hayom* (EXAMPLE 7.2b)[11] exemplifies the uninhibited Berdichev style of *Chazanut Haregesh*.

Example 7.2a employs a noble but austere melody which sweeps all before it, convincing through musical logic even as it keeps its listeners at a distance. It follows Western harmonic procedure, first modulating from B♭ minor to F minor at *yeichateimun* ('their fate is sealed'). Through an excursion to the dominant F major at *vechamah yibarei'un* ('and who shall enter the world'), it returns to B♭ minor at *mi yichyeh* ('who shall live'). Its chorale-like melody stems from six *Misinai* Tunes: $\boxed{21}$; $\boxed{28}$; $\boxed{34}$; $\boxed{13}$; $\boxed{35}$; and $\boxed{16}$, repeated and varied to fit the harmonic scheme.

Example 7.2b is unpredictable, slowly twining each phrase with tonal garlands before rising to an anguished climax at *kamah ya'avrun* ('who shall leave the world'). It descends resignedly, to a whispered *umi yamut* ('and who shall die'), by way of a typically Eastern European lowered-second degree, C♭. It too draws from the traditional stock, this time Lithuanian Biblical neume motifs. Fourteen in all, excluding repeats, they include seven HAF motifs, two each from TOR, HHD, and RES, and one from LAM (all listed above the music).

In one respect the Vienna-*Ritus Berosh Hashanah* (EXAMPLE 7.2c)[12] resembles the Odessa and Berdichev styles. It encourages congregational participation, but not the boisterous singing we have come to expect. *Berosh Hashanah* is a sublime meditation on the ineffable; musical settings for it are traditionally restrained, intended to resonate in the hearts—not the mouths—of listeners.

The motifs of Examples 7.2a–c are familiar, so that worshippers can move along with the cantor in an undertone. Gradually the undertone swells into a hum taken up by the congregation, until the whole synagogue is "in tune" with the song (see **PART II, CHAPTER TWO,** *The Congregational 'Drone')*. Approved for use in worship some 150 years ago with the proviso that no participant's voice be raised louder than that of the cantor,[13] Example 7.2c is still sung today in Vienna. The setting is rich in *Misinai* Tunes, those prime vehicles for the communal expression of Ashkenazic religious fervor (see **PART II, CHAPTER THREE,** *Misinai* **Tunes: Evolution**). The Tunes used here occur in almost every other HHD service: ⟦39⟧ , in Yom Kippur Eve; ⟦15⟧ , ⟦16⟧ , and ⟦27⟧ , in Shacharit; ⟦8⟧ , in Kedushah; ⟦28⟧ and ⟦23⟧ , in Musaf; ⟦3⟧ , in Maariv; ⟦5⟧ , in the Torah service; ⟦13⟧ in Kaddish; and ⟦34⟧ , in Selichot.

The Viennese Jewish community—then as now—came mostly from outside Vienna. To satisfy such a heterogenous congregation, Sulzer retained as many traditional motifs as possible within the parameters of Prayer-mode chant. Thus his *Berosh Hashanah* invites public participation without lowering the loftiness of its vision. I believe this is exactly the mix needed today in American synagogues, where Reform Judaism waited the better part of a century before admitting *Misinai* Tunes and Prayer modes into its service (see following Example).

Contrasted with Sulzer's version, the *Berosh Hashanah* offered in the *Union Hymnal* of 1932, composed by Samuel Naumbourg in 1847 (EXAMPLE 7.2d),[14] is an elongated, complex, and wide-ranging aria that lies well beyond a congregation's ability even to hum along. Notice how aloof it seems alongside the Vienna-*Ritus* style of Example 7.4c, although it uses five of the same *Misinai* Tunes— ⟦39⟧ , ⟦27⟧ , ⟦28⟧ , ⟦3⟧ , ⟦5⟧ , —and adds a sixth, ⟦2⟧ .

Nor has Sulzer's path been truly followed by Orthodox Judaism, which makes sporadic gestures in its direction; witness Moshe Koussevitsky's *Berosh Hashanah* (EXAMPLE 7.2e).[15] Faithful to the Vienna-*Ritus Misinai*-pattern through 11 measures, it deviates at ⟦5⟧ (*yibarei'un*), resolving to the upper—rather than lower—B♭. At *mi yichyeh* it abandons Selichah-*Techinah*, the mode of Pardon, and introduces *Ahavah Rabah*, the mode of Supplication (through motifs [1] and [1b], highly ornamented). Such post-Holocaust chazanic license is understandable: if forgiveness is inapplicable (of what sin were the six million European martyrs guilty?), let supplication beg mercy for their souls, in the same mode used to offer Memorial prayers. The congregation takes no more part in Orthodox solo emotionalism than it does in the formalism of classical Reform practice (Example 7.2d).

During the post-World War II years, Conservatism seemed poised to mediate between the formal and emotional approaches, showing the way in America as the Vienna *Ritus* had done in Europe a century before. Conservative cantors like David J. Putterman (1901–1979) of New York's Park Avenue Synagogue met the growing demand for congregational participation by interpolating adapted communal refrains into peak moments of the liturgy such as the *Berosh Hashanah* of EXAMPLE 7.2f.[16] The refrain in this case is not of one cloth with the ongoing music, albeit the same man, Zavel Zilberts (1881–1949), composed both. Putterman's choice for the congregational refrain paraphrases Zilberts' arrangement of a Shabbat *Zemirah* ('table song'; EXAMPLE 7.2g).[17]

> *Baruch eil elyon . . .*
> 'Blessed is God exalted, who gave rest to our souls, and relief from dismay and woe'.

True, the $^2_4$ *Allegretto* of Example 7.2g has been slowed to a $^4_4$ *Maestoso* in EXAMPLE 7.2f and the melody adjusted. Still, the refrain seems inappropriate to the liturgical moment. Its *ethos* has not changed: it remains a dance-tune, patched onto cantorial recitative that uses motifs of the Study, Ukranian-Dorian, Selichah-*Techinah*, and *Ahavah-Rabah* modes (as listed above the music).

A more appropriate refrain for the solo line of Example 74f, in Selichah-*Techinah*, is that shown in EXAMPLE 7.2h.[18] Composed for a Conservative service by Max Helfman (1901–1963), it develops *Misinai* Tune ⟨16⟩ in two different ways, resembling its Recurrence[19] and Primary Occurrence[20] in Appendix C.

Readers may wish to review the six approaches of Example 7.2, until the stylistic differences become clear. Whatever one's preferences, the fact that the settings were conceived within specific styles is what matters. "The dialogue between each great artist and history is conducted in his own language," writes André Malraux.[21] As performing artists cantors conduct their dialogue—with the God of History—in recognizable styles of chazanut, whether 'formal', 'emotional', or a mixture of both.

EXAMPLE 7.2

Six approaches to a prayer in 19th- and 20th-century Europe and America.

d. Reform Judaism (aloof Formalism)

f. Conservative Judaism (inappropriate Refrain)

Be - rosh ha-sha-nah yi - ka - tei-vun; yi-ka - tei - vun, uve-yom tsom kip-pur

CANTOR Study mode [15 – 1 – 3]

yei - cha-tei-mun; yei-cha-tei - mun. Be - rosh hashanah yikatei-vun,

Study mode [1 5 – 1 – 4 – 3]

uveyom tsom kippur yeicha-tei - mun, ka-mah ya'av-run, ve-chamah yiba-rei - un;

Ukranian-Dorian [2b] Selichah-*Techinah* [14] CONGREGATION:

ka - mah ya - av-run, vecha-mah _____ yiba-rei 3 - un. (Berosh . . .)

CANTOR: *Abavah Rabah* [1]

Mi yich - yeh, u - mi 3 ya 3 - mut.

g. Table-song origin of 7.2 Refrain

Allegretto

Original pitch

Ba - ruch_eil el - yon a - sher na-tan me - nu - chah, le - naf - shei-nu

fid - yom mi-sheit va'a - na - chah.

h. *Misinai*-based Refrain for Example 7.2

Largo

Original pitch

Be - rosh ha-sha-nah yika - tei - vun, uve-yom tsom kip - pur yeicha-tei - mun.

[16]

lechalot _____ ulcha-nein _ o - rot _____ mei - o - fel

[16](Recurrence in Appendix C) [16] (Primary Occurence in Appendix C)

EXAMPLE 7.2, *continued.*

Improvisation

Motivic Material

To understand improvising in a Prayer mode, think of waves as they break on shore: the crests are motifs; and the troughs, reciting-tones. We've already seen the six Prayer modes and their motifs.

PRINCIPAL MODES

1) *Adonai Malach*– [17] motifs–Example 5.6d
2) *Magein Avot*– [16] motifs–Example 5.9d
3) *Ahavah Rabah*– [11] motifs–Example 5.12d

SECONDARY MODES

4) Ukranian-Dorian–[2b in *Adonai Malach*]–Example 6.3a
                  [2b in *Magein Avot*]–Example 6.5a
                  [2b in *Ahavah Rabah*]–Example 6.5b
5) Study mode–   [2 motifs in *Adonai Malach*]–Example 6.6a
                  [2 motifs in *Magein Avot*]–Example 6.6b
                  [3 motifs in *Ahavah Rabah*]–Example 6.6c
                  [15 motifs in *Magein Avot*]–Example 6.7: a;b;c

6) THREE–PART SELICHAH MODE

Vidui-section–   [in *Adonai Malach*]– Example 6.9a
                  [in *Magein Avot*]–Example 6.9f
Nechamah-section – [in *Adonai Malach*]–Example 6.9b
                  [in combined *Magein Avot*/Study mode]
                  –Example 6.9c
                  [in combined *Magein Avot*/Ukranian-Dorian]
                  –Example 6.9d
                  [in combined *Adonai Malach*/*Magein Avot*]
                  –Example 6.9e
Techinah-section– [11 *Misinai* Tunes]–Example 6.14

The 44 Principal-mode motifs, added to the 33 Secondary-and-Selichah-mode motifs, plus mode-mixing and transposition (explained in the following subsection), offer unlimited possibilities.

Shifting Modes

Hashkiveinu is one of those 'breathing-space' liturgical passages which lends itself to modal inventiveness. EXAMPLE 7.3 takes one of its phrases, *Vehoshi'einu lema'an shemecha* ('Save us for thy name's sake'; Example 6.8a, Adolph Katchko's version, lines 3–4), and shifts it from *Ahavah Rabah* (EXAMPLE 7.3a) to *Magein Avot* (EXAMPLE 7.3b) and to *Adonai Malach* (EXAMPLE 7.3c). The tone density is typical of Psalmodic technique, ranging from syllabic (repeat of the word: *lema'an*) to melismatic (*Vehoshi'einu*). The phrasing flows; the modes are Principal Prayer modes in their "authentic" forms; all in all, a good way to begin improvising.

Note the changes in key signature as flats disappear from mode to mode: *Ahavah Rabah* has six flats; *Magein Avot* has but four; *Adonai Malach* keeps only two. But also note other pitch changes within each mode's motifs: *Ahavah Rabah* raises A♭ to A♮, creating the augmented second, A♮–G♭; *Magein Avot* lowers penultimate G to G♭ for Eastern European flavor; *Adonai Malach* twice changes E♭ to G (circled), a more typical rest-tone.

a. *Ahavah Rabah*

Vehoshi-ei - 6 - 6 - nu le-ma-an,— le-ma'an she-me-cha.

b. *Magein Avot*

Vehoshi-ei - 6 - 6 - nu le-ma-an,— le-ma'an she-me-cha.

c. *Adonai Malach*

Vehoshi-ei - 6 - 6 - nu le-ma-an,— le-ma'an she-me-cha.

EXAMPLE 7.3
Shifting a *Hashkiveinu*-phrase from *Ahavah Rabah* into
two different Principal Prayer modes, while retaining
Biblical tone density and "authentic" mode-form.

EXAMPLE 7.4 shifts another *Hashkiveinu*-phrase, *Vehagein ba'adeinu* ('Shield us from enemy, pestilence, sword, famine, and sorrow'), this time by Salomon Sulzer,[22] using neumatic tone density (typical of Biblical chant) and "plagal" forms of the three principal Prayer modes. EXAMPLE 7.4a gives the phrase in "plagal *Ahavah Rabah*; EXAMPLE 7.4b shifts it to "plagal" *Magein Avot*; EXAMPLE 7.4c shifts it to "plagal" *Adonai Malach*.

Again note the progressive disappearance of key-signature flats: *Ahavah Rabah* has six; *Magein Avot* has but five; *Adonai Malach* keeps only three. Apart from the raised D♭ (to D♮) in A*havah Rabah* (Example

7.4a, creating the augmented second, D♮–C♭, and the raised A♭ (to A♮) in *Adonai Malach* (Example 7.4c, creating the leading tone A♮–B♭), there are no other pitch changes within each mode's motifs.

EXAMPLE 7.4

Shifting another *Hashkiveinu*-phrase from *Ahavah Rabah* into two different Principal Prayer modes, while retaining Biblical tone density and "plagal" mode-form.

Shifting Texts

Not only can we sing a motivic pattern in several modes (Examples 7.3 and 7.4), using Psalmodic or Biblical technique and "authentic" or "plagal" mode-forms, we can also apply that pattern to a text different than the prayer for which the music was composed. Often a classic pattern like Pinchik's *Raza Deshabbat* (Example 5.2) goes unheard simply because its text does not appear in most Ashkenazic prayer books. Yet the mystical mood of its music (accompanying the words: 'When Sabbath arrives . . . in perfect union with the Heavenly King . . . the holy people are invested with new souls . . . now is the time to commence prayer') might beautifully intensify the text of the Shabbat Musaf introit, *Mi Shebeirach.*

Mi shebeirach avoteinu . . . hu yevareich. . .

'May He who blessed our forbears . . . bless
the people of this holy congregation, their
families, and all others who unite to pray:
those who found and maintain synagogues;
those who provide for transients; and those
who support the poor'.

*Vechol mi she'oskim . . . hakadosh
baruch hu . . .*

'May the Holy One, blessed be He, also bless
those who faithfully devote themselves to
communal needs. May He reward them,
preserve them in health, forgive their sins,
prosper their work, along with the work of all
Israel their brethren, and let us say, amen'.

EXAMPLE 7.5[23] reduces the music of Pinchik's *Raza Deshabbat* to
five phrases. Phrase **a–** features two reciting-tones, both on B♭. Phrase
b– uses two HAF neume motifs, *segol* and *revi'a*, and the B♭ reciting-
tones. Phrase **c–** combines two HHD neume motifs, *yetiv* and
munach, adding coloratura to a reciting-tone on the upper F. Phrase **d–**
repeats HHD *yetiv*, and ornaments it. Phrase **e–** fragments HHD
munach, and extends it into a cadence. Musical phrases **a–e** cover the
first paragraph of *Mi Shebeirach* and occupy lines 1–7 of Example 7.5,
leaving the second paragraph of *Mi Shebeirach* for the reader to fill in
with his or her own improvised music. The only variation occurs at the
second cadence, which should conclude with upper—rather than
lower—E♭–F.

EXAMPLE 7.5

Pinchik's *Raza Deshabbat* pattern.

Shifting Mode And Text

A Cantor should be capable of singing a motivic pattern in different Prayer modes as well as applying it to different texts. He or she should start with a simple piece, not too long (it's easy to expand musical ideas through reciting-tones, if needed). He or she will probably want to use an "authentic" Prayer mode, the most common form of chant. (A "plagal" section can always be added by moving the center of melodic activity up a fourth). Neume- or *Misinai*-derived motifs, not overly ornamented, are easiest (sustained final syllables achieve an attention-getting effect similar to ornamentation). Rest-and passing-tones should be adjusted to fit the new mode's motifs (consider the original pattern simply a theme for variation).

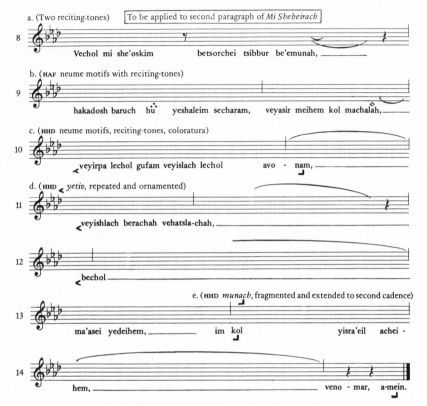

EXAMPLE 7.5, *continued.*

EXAMPLE 7.6a[24] presents a metrical setting of Psalm 81:1–4, recited every Thursday morning, as a pattern for improvisation, employing the rules-of-thumb stated above.

> *Harninu leilohim uzeinu . . .*
> 1. 'Sing aloud to God our strength;
> shout for joy to the God of Jacob!
> 2. Raise a song, sound the timbrel;
> the sweet lyre with the harp.
> 3. Blow the trumpet at the new moon;
> at the full moon, on our feast day.
> 4. For it is a statute for Israel;
> an ordinance of the God of Jacob'.

Marked "Majestically," the brief piece is in *Adonai Malach*, the Laudatory mode. Its eight *Adonai Malach* motifs: [1]; [1a]; [1b]; [2]; [2a]; [4]; [4a]; and [4b], plus Study-mode motif [5–1^1–5], are set in common time. A regular beat, though atypical of Weekday song, helps in memorizing motifs. The succeeding exercises—all in nonmetrical, semi-syllabic chant averaging between one and two notes per syllable—will test the reader's mastery of these nine motifs.

EXAMPLE 7.6b retains *Adonai Malach* as Prayer mode, but applies the Thursday-Psalm's motivic pattern to a Circumcision ceremony (*Berit Milah*).

> *Baruch atah, adonai . . .*
> 'Blessed art thou, O God, creator of the
> vine-fruit, who sanctified Israel, impressing
> thy statute in his flesh, marking his
> descendants with the holy covenant-sign. For
> thy covenant's sake, O God, deliver our loved
> ones from destruction'.

New rhythmic patterns—including occasional reciting-tones—loosen the Thursday-Psalm motifs' rigidity, approximating a cantor's habitual phrasing.

EXAMPLE 7.6c twice adds a tenth motif, Ukranian-Dorian [2b], but remains in the *Adonai Malach* mode. Such coloring of *Adonai Malach* is frequently done in retelling the Exodus story (Haggadah) on Passover Eve.

> *Avadim hayinu lefar'oh bemitsrayim . . .*
> 'We were once Pharoah's slaves in Egypt, but
> God brought us forth with a mighty hand and
> an outstretched arm [Deuteronomy 6:21;
> 26:8]. Had not God delivered our ancestors,
> then we and all our descendants might still
> be enslaved. Therefore, it is our duty to retell
> the story, at length'.

Observe how both Ukranian-Dorian motifs [2b] descend from the fifth degree of *Adonai Malach* (C), to its tonic (F), at *kulanu zekeinim* and at *vechol hamarbeh lesapeir bitsi'at mitsrayim*.

EXAMPLE 7.6d shifts the *Adonai Malach* pattern to a different mode, *Magein Avot*, and a different text, Genesis 2:1–3.

Vaichulu hashamayim veha'arets . . .
1. Thus the heavens and the earth were
finished; and all the host of them.
2. And on the seventh day God finished his
work which he had done; and he rested on
the seventh day from all the work which he
had done.
3. So God blessed the seventh day and
hallowed it; because on it God rested from all
his work which he had done in creation'.

Because of the mode change, motif numbers also change. For instance, the new equivalent of *Adonai Malach* opening motif [1b] (A–C–
D–C; line 1 in Example 7.6a) is *Magein Avot* motif [5b] (A♭–C–D♭–C;
line 1 in Example 7.6d). Five *Magein Avot* motifs appear in all: [5b]; [6];
[1a]; [4b]; and [4a]. In addition, Study-mode motif [15–1–3–1–15] (beginning and end of line 2) joins Study-mode motif [5–¹1–5] (middle of lines
1 and 3). Both are sung to the pitches of *Magein Avot* (tonic and fifth
degrees remain the same, but the third degree is lowered from A to A♭).
The bracketed numbers above the transposed motifs in Example 7.6d
are sung to the intervals of the Didactic mode. The five motifs, along
with two Study-mode motifs, make seven, one less than in the original
pattern of Example 7.6a.

EXAMPLE 7.6e moves between: two Principal modes (*Magein Avot*,
Adonai Malach); two Secondary modes (Study-mode, Ukranian-
Dorian); and incorporates nine reciting-tones (including those tied over
two staves). To lessen confusion, only the modes are indicated, rather
than individual motifs. The text is a Baraita (Babylonian Talmud,
treatise Berachot, 64a), sung at the conclusion of Musaf.

Amar rabi elazar, amar rabi chanina . . .
'Rabbi Elazar said in the name of Rabbi
Chanina, scholars [*bonayich,* or "thy
Builders"] increase peace throughout the
world, as it is written: Great shall be the
peace of thy builders. Abundant peace to all
lovers of thy torah . . . Peace be within thy
walls, security within thy palaces . . . The
Lord give strength to his people, and bless
them with peace'.

Observe how the mode-changes accommodate mood-changes in the text: *Shalom rav* ('Abundant peace'; middle of line 3) is sung to Study-mode motif [15–3–1–15] in the Didactic mode, *Magein Avot*, aptly portraying 'scholars'. At *toratecha* ('thy Torah'; the ensuing motif, line 3), the mode shifts to a bright *Adonai Malach*, alluding to TOR reading. Motif [4a] stems from [Lith]JUB/TOR *mercha sof-pasuk* ⁝ , used for the jubilatory reading of Song at the Sea (Exodus 15:1–21; Appendix B, line I TOR, group 11., motifs g–h). The voice should mirror each change.

EXAMPLE 7.6f, in the mode of Supplication, features six different *Ahavah Rabah* motifs: [1b]; [1]; [4]; [3]; [1c]; and [1a], plus Study-mode motif [5–1^1–5] and Ukranian-Dorian motif [2b]. The text of this Burial Service prayer is from Proverbs 31:10–16.

> *Eishet chayil mi yimtsah . . .*
> 10. 'A good wife who can find?
> she is far more precious than jewels.
> 11. The heart of her husband trusts in her;
> and he will have no lack of gain.
> 12. She does him good, and not harm;
> all the days of her life.
> 13. She seeks wool and flax;
> and works with willing hands.
> 14. She is like the ships of the merchant;
> she brings her food from afar.
> 15. She rises while it is yet night
> and provides food for her household;
> and tasks for her maidens.
> 16. She considers a field and buys it;
> with the fruit of her hand she plants a
> vineyard'.

Note how the solemn prosody causes Ukranian-Dorian motif [2b] to recur four times in a row, beginning with *Darsha tsemer* ('She seeks wool'; middle of line 3), and continuing through the next three descriptive phrases: . . . 'willing hands'; ' . . . ships of the merchant'; ' . . . food from afar' (middle of line 3 and all of line 4). The Ukranian-Dorian recurrences establish a far-away mood that fits the final tribute.

EXAMPLE 7.6g employs our by-now-familiar pattern, among *Ahavah Rabah*, Study mode, *Adonai Malach*, and Ukranian-Dorian. If we remove Study-mode motif [5–1^1–5] from the end of line 1 (*adonai*; 'God') and Ukranian-Dorian motif [2b] from the end of line 4 (*liheyot lachem leilohim*; 'that He is our God'), this recalls Example 6.2a, Sulzer's rendition of the same Musaf Kedushah text.

> *Shema, yisra'eil . . . hu eloheinu . . .*
> 'Hear, O Israel: The Lord our God is one Lord
> . . . He is our God, our Father, our King, our
> Saviour; and He in his mercy will again
> proclaim to us, in the presence of all living,
> that He is our God'.

Unlike Sulzer's version—which we have deciphered as being entirely in *Ahavah Rabah*—Example 7.6g reveals both sides of the modal coin: darkness and light; supplication and praise. Still, a "caressing" quality suits both illustrations.

EXAMPLE 7.6h—the last in this series of shifts—visits every Principal and Secondary mode, plus the *Techinah*-section of the Selichah mode, at least twice. The modal sequence (not counting recurrences) is: *Magein Avot*; Study mode; Ukranian-Dorian; Selichah-*Techinah*; *Adonai Malach*; and *Ahavah Rabah*.

To accommodate the "plagal" Selichah-*Techinah* motif-sequence (last half of line 3; first half of line 4), Example 7.6h moves its tonic up from *Magein Avot* $\underline{F}$ to Selichah-*Techinah* $\underline{B\flat}$. Remaining on a "plagal"-$B\flat$ pitch-level, it immediately repeats the motif-sequence (see motifs [1]–[4b]–[1a]; line 3 of Example 7.6a) in *Adonai Malach*, raising $\underline{D\flat}$ to $\underline{D\natural}$ and lowering $\underline{E}$ to $\underline{E\flat}$. On line 7, it repeats the same motif-sequence, this time in a "plagal"-minor Study mode with $\underline{F}$ as tonic (in other words, "plagal" *Magein Avot*, with Study-mode motif [15–1–3–1–15] ($\underline{1C}$–$\underline{F}$–$\underline{A\flat}$–$\underline{F}$–$\underline{1C}$).

The text of Example 7.6h, an extended paragraph necessitating the above melody-stretching devices, is from Festival Musaf.

> *Eloheinu veilohei avoteinu . . . melech
> rachaman,*
> 'Our God and God of our forbears, merciful
> King, have mercy upon us; Beneficent One,
> hear our entreaty. Return to us for the sake of
> our ancestors who performed thy will; rebuild
> thy Temple on its former site, and grant that we
> may be gladdened by its restoration. Return
> Priest and Levite to their former duties, and
> Israel to its land. There may we again worship
> before thee during our Pilgrimage festivals:
> Pesach; Shavuot; and Sukkot'.

EXAMPLE 7.6

Shifting a metrical motivic pattern (Psalm 81) to seven other modes and texts,
all in semi-syllabic chant.

c. Passover Haggadah (*Adonai Malach* mode, plus Study-mode motif [5–1[1]–5] and Ukranian-Dorian motif [2b])

Ava - dim hayinu lefar'oh bemitsrayim, vayotsi'ei - nu adonai eloheinu misham beyad chazakah___

uvizro - a_ ne-tu-yah. Ve-i - lu__ lo ho-tsi hakadosh baruch hu et avoteinu mimitsra - yim,

harei a-nu uva-nei-nu uvenei va-nei-nu, meshuba-dim ha-yi-nu lefar-oh bemits-ra - yim.

Va'a - fi - lu ku-la-nu chachamim, ___ ku-la-nu zekei-nim, ___

ku - la - nu yode-im et hato-rah,_ mits-vah a-lei - nu lesa-peir bi-tsi-at mits-ra-yim.

Vechol hamar-beh lesa-peir bitsi-at mits-ra - yim harei zeh__ meshu-bach. ___

d. Friday Night Maariv (*Magein Avot* mode, plus Study-mode motifs [5–1[1]–5] and [1 5–1–3–1 5])

1. Vai - chu-lu hasha-ma-yim ve - ha - a-rets ve-chol_ tseva - am.

2. Vai - chal elohim bayom hashvi-i me-lach-to a-sher_ a-sah, _ vayishbot bayom hashvi' i

3. mikol me-lach-to asher a-sah. Vai-va-rech elo-him ___ et yom hash-vi - i

4. vai ka - deish ___ o - to ki vo ___ sha-vat mi-kol ___

5. me - lach - to_ a - sher ba - ra_ elo - him la - a - sot.

e. Musaf conclusion: Two Principal modes (*Magein Avot* and *Adonai Malach*), two Secondary modes
(Study mode and Ukranian-Dorian), plus nine reciting-tones

f. Burial service (*Ahavah Rabah* mode, plus Study-mode motif [5–1¹–5] and Ukranian-Dorian motif [2b])

g. Musaf Kedushah (*Abavah Rabah,* Study mode, *Adonai Malach,* Ukranian-Dorian)

h. Festival Musaf (*Magein Avot,* Study mode, Ukranian-Dorian, Selichah-*Techinah, Adonai Malach, Abavah Rabah*)

EXAMPLE 7.6, *continued.*

At mention of the Pilgrimage festivals in Example 7.6h (line 12: *be-chag hamatsot; uvechag hashavu'ot; uvechag hasukkot*) three prescribed motifs appear, one for each of the Pilgrimage Festivals. We will now examine them further.

Prescribed Motifs

Seasonal

Five prescribed motifs herald various seasons of the liturgical year by appearing unannounced in the ongoing chant of: the three Pilgrimage Festivals; a minor festival (Chanukah); and a fast day (Tishah B'av). We have already encountered the first three of these motifs in the final line of Example 7.6h. There they alluded—en masse—to Pesach (Passover), Shavuot (Pentecost), and Sukkot (Tabernacles), in the Festival Musaf sung on all three occasions. EXAMPLES 7.7a,[25] 7.7b,[26] and 7.7c[27] cite the same motifs, here sung in the Hallel for Festival Schacharit; only the motif appropriate to the season is sung in each case.

> *Ana adonai . . .*
> 'Save us, we beseech thee, O Lord!'
> [Psalm 118:25].

Each seasonal motif can also be sung to the words of Kaddish for Festival Maariv (Example 7.1b; middle of line 1).

> *. . . be'olma di vera*
> ' . . . in the world which he has created'.

EXAMPLE 7.7d[28] is sung to the best-known 'Zion' poem composed by Judah Halevi (1075–1141), *Eli Tsiyon*. It is recited on the eve of Tishah B'av (the Ninth of Av), a midsummer day of mourning commemorating the sack of both Temples and numerous other catastrophes.

> *Eli Tsiyon ve'areha . . .*
> 'Weep for Zion and her cities . . . weep for her
> ruined Temple . . . and for the blood that was
> spilled'.

The Study-session Kaddish recited during Tishah B'av Shacharit is a good spot to insert this motif, at the words *be'olma di vera* (Example 7.1e; end of line 1 and beginning of line 2).

EXAMPLE 7.7e[29] initiates a 13th-century hymn, *Ma'oz Tsur*, the name of whose author is unknown, but whose English rendering is famous (the opening letter of each Hebrew stanza spells out the unknown author's first name acrostically: Mord'chai).

> Rock of Ages, let our song
> praise thy saving power;
> thou amidst the raging foes,
> wast our shel'tring tower.[30]

Ma'oz Tsur is sung as part of a Candle-lighting ceremony on Chanukah, the early-winter festival celebrating Maccabean restoration of the Second Temple in –165. An excellent place to interpolate the motif is Kaddish for Friday Night Maariv of the Festival week. Its appearance is usually delayed until the second phrase, *be'olma di vera* (Example 7.1d; middle of line 1). This achieves maximum surprise since worshippers, anticipating the normal Sabbath chant, will instead 'round the corner' into Chanukah-awareness.

EXAMPLE 7.7
Five seasonal motifs.

Paragraph Openings and Closing Blessings

Other prescribed motifs, which open and close the paragraphs of every liturgical section, 'tag' various services throughout the year. EXAMPLE 7.8 shows 10 prescribed Paragraph-opening and Closing-blessing motifs that appear in almost every service: weekday; Sabbath; Festival; and High Holy Day. Paragraph-opening texts vary with the occasion but Closing blessings all begin with the formula,

> *Baruch atah, adonai . . .*
> 'Blessed art Thou, O Lord',

and then continue with a particular blessing-text, such as *mekadeish hashabbat* ('Hallower of the Sabbath'; Friday Night Kiddush). Together with the five prescribed seasonal motifs of Example 7.7, the 10 motifs of Example 7.8 provide musical landmarks for cantors and worshippers. Diagonal double lines (//) separate Paragraph openings from Closing blessings in both text and music.

EXAMPLE 7.8a,[31] from the Amidah of Weekday Shacharit and Minchah, features the "plagal" motifs of *Adonai Malach*, a mode normally considered "authentic," moving between its tonic, A♭, and the fifth below, E♭.

Refa'einu, adonai, veneirafei . . . / /
Baruch atah . . . rofei cholei amo yisra'eil
'Heal us, O Lord, and we shall be healed . . . / /
Blessed art Thou . . . Healer of the Sick'.

EXAMPLE 7.8b,[32] from Weekday Maariv, shows "authentic" *Ahavah Rabah* motifs moving between the mode's tonic, E, to almost an octave above. The normally-raised third degree, G♯, is lowered to G♮ only for the blessing formula.

Umalchuto beratson kiblu aleihem . . . / /
Baruch atah . . . ga'al yisra'eil
'He whose children willingly accepted his
sovereignty . . . / /
Blessed art Thou . . . Redeemer of Israel'.

EXAMPLE 7.8c,[33] from Friday Night Maariv, uses "plagal" Selichah-*Techinah* motifs moving between the fifth below and third above the tonic, B♭. The seventh and sixth degrees are almost always raised a half-step, to A♮ and G♮, respectively.

Uma'avir yom umeivi lailah, umavdil
bein yom uvein lailah . . . / /
Baruch atah . . . hama'ariv aravim
'Thou causest day to pass and night to come, distinguishing between night and darkness . . . / /
Blessed art Thou . . . Bringer of Evening'.

EXAMPLE 7.8d,[34] from the Amidah for Shabbat Shacharit or Musaf, is in "authentic" *Ahavah Rabah*, but at a higher pitch (tonic, G) than Weekday Maariv Example 7.7b (tonic, E). The higher pitch imparts a 'ring' to the voice, appropriate to the more elaborate Sabbath ritual, with its congregational hymns, Torah and Haftarah readings, and sermon.

Eloheinu veilohei avoteinu . . . / /
Baruch atah . . . mekadeish hashabbat
'Our God and God of our forbears . . . / /
Blessed art Thou . . . Hallower of Sabbath'.

EXAMPLE 7.8e,[35] from the Amidah of Shabbat Minchah, follows "authentic" Study-mode patterns in the *Magein Avot* mode, but lowers the second degree, G̲, to G̲♭ in its Closing-blessing formula.

Ledor vador nagid godlecha . . . / /
Baruch atah . . . ha'eil hakadosh
'Through all generations we declare thy
greatness . . . / /
Blessed art Thou . . . O Holy God'.

EXAMPLE 7.8f,[36] from Festival Maariv, combines "authentic" *Magein Avot* in its Paragraph opening with "plagal" Selichah-*Techinah* in its Closing blessing. Interestingly, opening *Magein Avot* uses lower D̲ as "authentic" tonic, while closing Selichah-*Techinah* uses upper D̲ as "plagal" tonic.

Venismach bedivrei toratecha
uvemitsvotecha le'olam va'ed . . . / /
Baruch atah . . . oheiv amo yisra'eil
'We rejoice in the words of thy Torah and in
thy precepts forevermore . . . / /
Blessed art Thou . . . Lover of Israel'.

EXAMPLE 7.8g,[37] from the Amidah of Festival Shacharit, Musaf, and Minchah, juggles two modes: "plagal" Selichah-*Techinah*; and "authentic" Study mode, both using A̲ as tonic. It blurs the division between the two modes by varying pitches within its Paragraph-opening motif. Thus Example 7.8g gives two versions of the first word, **Vehasi'einu.**

Version I is sung to *Misinai* Tune ⟨17⟩ (Example 3.11, Prayer–type IIg, *Me'orah*; 'Concerning "The Creator of Light" ', and Appendix C, left–hand column); version II is in "plagal" Selichah-*Techinah*, with the seventh degree raised a half-step, to G̲♯. Thereafter, G̲♮ (lowered seventh degree) indicates an "authentic" Study mode.

Line 2 offers another option: Ukranian-Dorian motif [2b] may appear, at ***mo'adecha***, by raising D̲ to D̲♯. The key words for both options are in bold type.

> **Vehasi'einu**, *adonai eloheinu,*
> *et birkat **mo'adecha** ... //*
> 'O God, bestow on us thy Festival
> blessings ... //
> 'Blessed art Thou ... Hallower of Festivals'.

EXAMPLE 7.8h,[38] from High Holy Day Maariv, lies firmly within "authentic" *Adonai Malach* on D, paraphrasing motifs [1b] and [1c] in its Paragraph opening (refer to chart in Example 5.5d). This Example, most typical of German *chazanut*, cites the same text as Example 7.8c, which is equally representative of Lithuanian *chazanut*.

> *Uma'avir yom umeivi lailah ... //*
> *Baruch atah ... hama'ariv aravim*
> 'Thou causest day to pass and night to
> come ... //
> Blessed art Thou ... Bringer of Evening'.

EXAMPLE 7.8i,[39] from High Holy Day Shacharit, mixes two modes: it opens and closes in "plagal" Selichah-*Techinah* on A; yet its second motif (*kumah be'ezrat yisra'eil*) is in "authentic" *Adonai Malach* on C.

> *Tsur yisra'eil, kumah be'ezrat yisra'eil ... //*
> *Baruch atah ... ga'al yisra'eil*
> 'O Israel's Rock, arise and deliver Israel ... //
> Blessed art thou ... Israel's Deliverer'.

EXAMPLE 7.8j,[40] from the Amidah of every High Holy Day service, is in a straightforward, "authentic" *Magein Avot* mode on F, considered the 'High Holy Day Mode' par excellence.

> *Vetimloch, atah adonai, levadecha, al*
> *kol ma'asecha ... //*
> *Baruch atah ... hamelech hakadosh*
> 'Thou alone shalt reign, O Lord, over all thy
> works ... //
> Blessed art Thou ... O Holy King'.

EXAMPLE 7.8
Ten Paragraph-opening and Closing-Blessing motifs
that "tag" services throughout the year.

EXAMPLE 7.8, *continued.*

The ten Paragraph-opening and Closing-blessing excerpts of Example 7.8 cut to the very sinew of Synagogue song, embodying every Prayer mode in either its "authentic" or "plagal" form. Why do "authentic" motifs seem Apollonian or 'formal', while "plagal" motifs seem Dionysian or 'emotional'? Perhaps it has to do with the difference between a forthright, open ascent (1–3–5) in "authentic" motifs and a flanking, semi-closed one (₁5–3–1) in "plagal" motifs. The former is predictable and therefore, formal, while the latter is unexpected and so, more emotional. For instance, Weekday-Shacharit/Minchah Example 7.8a, in "plagal" *Adonai Malach*, lends itself to emotional rendition, while Weekday-Maariv Example 7.8b, in "authentic" *Ahavah Rabah*, works better when sung formally.

Of late, ethnic awareness among fourth-generation American Jews has weakened, and not only Prayer modes, but also prescribed Seasonal, Paragraph-opening, and Closing-blessing motifs are fading as well. Sameness has crept into the services of all three movements, making it difficult to distinguish one occasion from another. This, plus the inhibiting tendency of amplification (see **Vocal Quality** subsection, this chapter) and rabbinical insistence on "participation" by an indifferent laity, have had a stultifying effect on Synagogue song in America. How this situation developed and what is being done to improve it are recounted in the next chapter.

Vocal Quality; Style; Improvisation; Prescribed Motifs: Bibliography & Notes

1. KATZ, Sholom: *Kol Nidre* and Yom Kippur Service, New York, Westminster (1958), recording XWN 18858, side one, band nine; transcribed by Joseph A. Levine.
2. BAER, Abraham: *Baal T'fillah*, Gothenburg, published by the author (1877), number 758a.
3. WODAK, Meyer: *Hamnazeach*, Vienna, published by the author, (1897), after number 223.
4. TALMON, Zvi: *Rinat Hahechal*, New York, Cantors Assembly (1965), after pages 55–57.
5. LEVINE, Joseph A.: *Emunat Abba* (Baltimore Hebrew College, 1981), Ann Arbor, University Microfilms, Volume II, number 378.
6. KWARTIN, Zavel: *Smiroth Zebulon*, New York, published by the author (1928), number 48.
7. PARKIN, P.H., H.R. Humphreys, & J.R. Cowell: *Acoustics, Noise, and Buildings*, London, Faber (1979), page 97.
8. FORSYTH, Michael: *Buildings for Music*, Cambridge, Massachusetts Institute of Technology (1985), pages 3–9.
9. VIGODA, Samuel: *Legendary Voices*, New York, M.P. Press (1981), page 53.
10. BLUMENTHAL, Nisi: "Shivisi," *Cantorial Anthology*, edited by Gershon Ephros, New York, Bloch (1940), Volume II, pages 231–232.
11. BELZER, Nisi: "Hayom Haras Olom," *A Song Treasury of Old Israel*, edited by Lazare Saminsky, New York, Bloch (1951), pages 8–9.
12. SULZER, Salomon: *Schir Zion* (Vienna, 1839–1865), reissued by Joseph Sulzer, Vienna (1905), number 354.

13. GRUNWALD, Max: *Vienna*, translated by Solomon Grayzel, Philadelphia, Jewish Publication Society (1936), page 220; by Imperial decree, all congregational tunes had to be kept on file in the Municipal Archives.
14. NAUMBOURG, Samuel: "Berosh Hashanah" (Paris, 1847, number 255), *Union Hymnal*, Cincinnati, Central Conference of American Rabbis (1932), number 328.
15. KOUSSEVITSKY, Moshe: *From the Repertoire of Cantor Moshe Koussevitsky*, New York, Tara (1977), page 26.
16. ZILBERTS, Zavel: "B'rosh Hashonoh," *Mizmor L'david*, edited by David J. Putterman, New York, Cantors Assembly (1979), pages 240–242.
17. ZILBERTS, Zavel: *Zmiros*, New York, Katz (1923), page 2.
18. HELFMAN, Max: "Berosh Hashanah," *Music at Congregation Rodeph Sholom*, New York, Congregation Rodeph Sholom (1980), recording, side 2, band 3; transcribed by Joseph A. Levine (originally composed for Congregation B'nai Abraham of Newark).
19. GEROVITCH, Eliezer: *Shirei Tefilah*, Rostow-on-Don, published by the author (1890), number 30.
20. BAER (see item 2), number 1022a.
21. MALRAUX, André: *The Voices of Silence*, translated by Stuart Gilbert, Princeton, Princeton University (1978), page 413.
22. SULZER (see item 12), number 39; slightly altered for Example 76a.
23. PINCHIK, Pierre: "Rozo D'shabos," *The Repertoire of Hazzan Pinchik*, New York, Cantors Assembly (1964), pages 78–88, adapted.
24. LEWY, Michael David: "Psalm for Thursday." *Daily Psalms*, Tel Aviv, Hapoel Hamizrachi (1954), page 3.
25. BAER (see item 2), number 820a.
26. BAER (see item 2), number 820b.
27. BAER (see item 2), number 820c:2.
28. IDELSOHN, Abraham Zvi: *Jewish Music*, New York, Holt (1929), page 168:9.
29. IDELSOHN (see item 28), page 168:10.
30. JASTROW, M., & G. Gottheil: "Rock of Ages," *Sabbath and Festival Prayer Book*, New York, Rabbinical Assembly (1973), page 365.
31. LEVINE (see item 5), number 185.
32. WOHLBERG, Max: *Arvit L'ḥol*, Elkins Park, PA, Ashbourne (1972), pages 6–8.
33. KATCHKO, Adolph: *Thesaurus of Cantorial Liturgy*, New York, Hebrew Union College (1952), after number 32.
34. SULZER (see item 12), number 88.
35. ROTHSTEIN, Arnold: *Minchah Leshabbat*, New York, Yeshiva University (1954), page 2.
36. ALTER, Israel: *The Festival Service*, New York, Cantors Assembly (1969), after page 5.
37. BAER (see item 2), after numbers 789–803.

38. NAUMBOURG, Samuel: *Zemirot Yisra'eil*, Paris, published by the author (1847), number 191.
39. SCHORR, Baruch: *N'ginoth Baruch Schorr*, edited by Israel Schorr, New York, Bloch (1928), number 81.
40. LEWANDOWSKY, Louis: *Kol Rinnah U'tfillah*, Berlin, published by the author (1871), after numbers 167–168.

CHAPTER EIGHT

The Americanization of Synagogue Song: A Survey

Diaspora *chazanut* always interacts with its host culture. Among the various waves of Jewish immigration to America, however, Eastern Ashkenazic ethnicity has exerted the strongest influence. Its Slavic/Oriental song pervades even the Protestantized Reform ritual, in the form of neo-Chasidic refrains. These, plus indigenous American motifs, are opening new paths to a younger generation.

Seventeenth and Eighteenth Centuries

American *chazanut* got its start in 1654, when the Inquisition drove 23 Marranos (supposedly Christianized Jews) from Spanish Brazil to Dutch New Amsterdam in what is now the state of New York. The Synagogue song of the Marranos and their descendants mirrored their Western Sephardic heritage, specifically the Amsterdam-London rite which survived the 1492–1498 expulsions from Spain and Portugal. That rite—known as the London Minhag—is austere and measured, sung with precision by the entire congregation. For instance, most diaspora communities apply the *darga* and *tevir* motifs (bracketed) of EXAMPLE 8.1 to the Bible reading of Torah or Ruth-Ecclesiastes-Song of Solomon (see Example 4.5a and Appendix C ⎡21⎤, right-hand column). EXAMPLE 8.1a[1] shows those motifs in the London-Minhag congregational tune for Song at the Sea (Exodus 15:1–21), as it appears in Shacharit prayer.

> . . . . *et hashirah hazot ladonai* . . . / /
> 1. '[Then Moses . . . sang] this song' . . . / /
> . . . *ozi vezimrat yah*
> 2. 'The Lord is my strength and my song'.

EXAMPLE 8.1b,[2] another London-Minhag congregational song, is for an *Akeidah*-type Piyyut, or 'Poem on the Binding of Isaac', by Judah Samuel Abbas (died in Aleppo, Syria, 1167). It, too, uses the universal *darga* and *tevir* motifs (bracketed) in stately congregational song.

> *Al har asher kavod* . . .
> 'Upon a mountain radiant with God's glory,
> stand the binder [Abraham], the one who is
> bound [Isaac], and the altar'!

a. Moses' Song at the Sea

1....et hashi - rah ha- zot _____ lado - nai _____ 2. O - zi ve - zimrat yah

b. Poem on the Binding of Isaac

Al har _____ a - sher - ka - vod le - cha - zo - rei - ach,

o - keid ve - ha - ne'e - kad ve - ha - - - miz - bei - ach.

EXAMPLE 8.1
The Sephardic London Minhag, incorporating neume motifs *darga*
and *tevir* in Shacharit prayer.

Early Sephardic congregations include: Shearith Israel (New York City, 1655); Jeshuath Israel (Newport, RI, 1658); Mikveh Israel (Savannah, GA, 1735); Mikveh Israel (Philadelphia, PA, 1747); and Beth Elohim (Charleston, SC, 1749). After 1700 the Ashkenazic component of Jewry grew in America, leaving Sephardic Jews a proud but isolated minority. But Ashkenazic practice treats music less rigidly than the Sephardic London Minhag, allowing worshippers to recite most prayers in an undertone, with the cantor improvising Paragraph openings and Closing blessings (based on prescribed motifs listed in Example 7.8a–j). Such dependence upon improvisation—in the absence of a well–trained cantorate—left no musical trail of early Ashkenazic practice in America.

Congregations during the late-17th and early-18th centuries followed the structure of all religious denominations in this country, but especially that of the dominant group, Protestantism. Instead of a governmentally organized religious community to which local branches might be held accountable, as in Europe, Jewish immigrants found a system of separately equal, autonomous sects. For the first time in the long history of the diaspora, individual congregations in America determined their own rites free of a hierarchical superstructure.[3]

Nineteenth Century

The 19th-century pattern is one of minorities within congregations resigning over ritual issues, Ashkenazic versus Sephardic at first, Reform versus Orthodox later on. At the time of the early splits (1801–1825) there were about 10,000 Jews scattered throughout the United States. Each community constituted an independent congregation which set its own religious standards, much like the isolated towns of Colonial New England. Synagogues had no pulpits and did not employ preaching rabbis. The office of spiritual leader was filled by a cantor who functioned as a minister by law. Gershom Mendes Seixas (1745–1816), the first American-born chazan (as the cantor is still called in Sephardic congregations) and a Trustee of Columbia University, carried the title *Pontifex Judearum*.

But chazanic ministerial function proved at best a stop-gap. Although communities required a *Sheli'ach Tsibbur*, or 'Messenger-in-Prayer', to hold worship services, most qualified cantors refused to leave Europe for an uncertain life in the New World. Those who came were generally unversed in Jewish Law; the only requirement they fulfilled was possessing "a pleasant voice" (Babylonian Talmud, treatise Ta'anit, or "Fasts', 16a). As public worship suffered, critics began blaiming cantor-ministers for all the evils that beset American synagogues, from lack of decorum to lack of spiritual content.[4]

In 1840 the first ordained rabbi, Abraham Rice (1802–1862) of Bavaria, came to Congregation Nidche Israel in Baltimore. His arrival heralded a steady immigration of German Jews who would eventually transform American Jewish society from isolated congregationalist communities into nationally organized denominations. The process began in 1848 with modifications in ritual: spoken prayer took the place of chant, a rabbi-reader took the place of the cantor, services were shortened, and *piyyutim* and *selichot* eliminated (see **CHAPTER THREE, *Misinai* Tunes: Evolution**).

Progressive congregations associated themselves with the emerging Reform Movement. Begun in Seesen, Westphalia in 1810, Reform Judaism flourished in the United States; American tolerance for all religious groups meshed with the Reformers' program of multiple Judaisms, i.e., Liberal along with Traditional. The Union of American Hebrew Congregations organized in 1874 and Hebrew Union College opened its doors in 1875.

Synagogues not yet ready to discard their traditionalist image formed the Conservative Movement, founding the Jewish Theological Seminary in 1877 and the United Synagogue in 1913. Orthodoxy established the Isaac Elchanan Theological Seminary in 1897 and the Union of Orthodox Jewish Congregations in 1898.

In the middle of the nineteenth century regular choirs began to supplant the occasional ones that had earlier appeared only at synagogue consecrations such as that of Shearith Israel (New York City, 1818). Many congregations installed organs to support the choral singing during worship, beginning with Beth Elohim (Charleston, SC, 1838). *A cappella* Synagogue music typically came from Vienna (EXAMPLE 8.2a)[5] and Paris (EXAMPLE 8.2b).[6] The 12th-century text of Example 8.2a imitates Arabic *hazag* meter (half-short-short-long syllables), yet its 19th-century tune is in $\frac{3}{4}$ time, Vienna-waltz style.

Adon olam asher malach . . .

'Eternal God who antedated
every living thing,
acclaimed by all which he created
to be the sov'reign King'.

The text of Example 8.2b is Biblical (Psalm 29:2–3), linking parallel ideas of 21 syllables (Congregation) and 14 syllables (Cantor) into a Golden Section proportion of 3:2 (refer to **PART I, JERUSALEM OF OLD: Nature of Second-temple Song**). However, its symmetrical, French-operetta style melody equalizes the two uneven verses. The Hebrew 21–to–14 ratio, unfortunately, vanishes in translation.

> *Havu ladonai kevod shemo . . .*
> 2. 'Ascribe to the Lord the glory
> of his name,
> worship the Lord in holy array.
> 3. The voice of the Lord is
> upon the waters,
> the God of glory thunders'.

EXAMPLE 8.2
19th-century Synagogue music from Vienna and Paris.

Pursuit of economic opportunity swelled the Jewish population to 200,000 by 1860. Mostly Germans, their aim was to Americanize themselves as rapidly as possible. It was an easy step to equate Americanism with its dominant religious tradition, Protestantism. By 1870 an Industrial-Age Elitism, patterned after the Southern pre-Civil War division between landowners and squatters, prevailed.[7] Transposed to an urban industrial setting, this two-tiered social structure was anything but egalitarian. Factory-owner Church trustees imported well-known ministers who preached to masses of worker-parishioners. Soon synagogues followed church architecture in emphasizing the preaching-pulpit, and Jewish services aped the Protestant practice of stressing the sermon. Congregational participation in both synagogue and church consisted of hymn-singing.

The Romantic melody of EXAMPLE 8.3,[8] using call-and-response between cantor and congregation, is typical of late-19th century synagogue hymnody, with organ accompaniment.

Ein Keiloheinu, ein kadoneinu . . .
'None is like our God, none like our Lord;
none like our King, none like our Redeemer'.

EXAMPLE 8.3
Call-and-response treatment of a hymn, with organ accompaniment.

The Cantorate: Nineteenth Century

The first full-time professional cantors brought over from Europe were: G.M. Cohen (Emanu-el, New York, 1845); Jacob Fraenkel (Rodeph Sholom, Philadelphia, 1848); Leon Sternberger (Anshe Chesed, New York, 1849); Ignatius Ritterman (B'nei Jeshurun, New York, 1855); Samuel Welsh (Ahavas Chesed, New York, 1865); Alois Kaiser (Ohev Sholom, Baltimore, 1866); and Moritz Goldstein (B'nei Israel, Cincinnati, 1881).

The American cantor's role would change radically during the century's second half. In 1849 he was still required to "chant in the ancient traditional style," according to the minutes of New York City's Congregation Emanu-El. Two years later Rabbi Isaac Mayer Wise (1819–1900), the 'father' of American Reform, abolished the office of chazan at Anshe Emeth Temple in Albany, NY. Instead, Rabbi Wise read both prayer and Scripture, a radical departure which put Synagogue song on hold in American Reform temples for the better part of a century.

The four techniques of *chazanut* that this book explains at length— Psalmodic, Biblical, Performance, and Modal—stem from the ancient first fruits of Israel's religious awakening. The classic texts, codified into Scripture and Prayer book as the written record of living speech, were always sung, never read. The form that this singing took—sacred chant—evolved over two millenia and perfectly suited its Hebrew liturgy.

When Rabbi Wise excised *chazanut* he effectively changed the language of prayer in American Reform temples. To replace Hebrew liturgical chant, he and other Reform rabbis published a series of hymnals, using predominantly German and English texts. As there existed no music for the newly-created hymn-texts, the *Union Hymnal* of 1897 borrowed melodies from oratorio, folksong, and Christmas carols: "I Know That My Redeemer Liveth" (hymn #3); "Auld Lang Syne" (hymn #80); "Deutschland über alles" (hymn #95); and "Hark! The Herald Angels Sing" (part II, hymn #8).

Two Reform organist-choirmasters composed their own music to the new texts, borrowing freely from operatic themes: Sigmund Schlesinger (1835–1906) of Mobile; and Max Spicker (1856–1912) of New York City. Three Reform cantors: Alois Kaiser (1840–1908) of Baltimore; Samuel

Welsh (1835–1901) of New York City; and Moritz Goldstein (1840–1906) of Cincinnati, collaborated in producing a four-volume liturgical anthology, *Zimrath Yah* (New York, 1871–1886). It did not take root, nor did the efforts of Edward Stark (1863–1918) of San Fransisco.

The Cantorate: Early Twentieth Century

In the wake of Russian persecutions after 1880, an influx of two million largely Traditional Eastern European Jews began, which served as counterweight to some of American Reform's Liberal excesses. Among the first Orthodox cantors to take up synagogue posts in New York were: Boruch Schorr (Mogen Avrohom, 1891); Alter Karniol (Ohab Zedek, 1893); Pinchos Minkowsky (Adath Jeshurun, 1897); and Israel Cooper (Kalvarier, 1900).

After World War I, with the impoverishment of European communities, more top-notch Traditional cantors fled to the United States, prompting claims of a Golden Age: Zeidel Rovner and Yossele Rosenblatt (1912); Aryeh Rutman and Berele Chagy (1913); Samuel Malavsky (1914); Jacob Beimel (1916); David Roitman, Zavel Kwartin, Herman Semiatin, Joseph Shlisky, and Abba Weisgal (1920); Mordechai Hershman and Adolph Katchko (1921); Samuel Vigoda (1923); David Steinberg and Israel Schorr (1924); Pierre Pinchik (1925); Leib Glantz (1926).

Cantorial recitatives of that era are typically virtuosic. Phonograph recordings 'froze' immensely popular prayer-interpretations, encouraging every would-be cantor to parody salient features, stifling potential for variant treatments of the same texts.[9] Moreover, cantors recorded only set pieces—those rare static moments during the service—while neglecting the fluidity that was the hallmark of their practice.

One such static piece, *Hashkiveinu* (EXAMPLE 8.4),[10] was published in 1927 by the celebrated "King of Cantors," Yossele Rosenblatt. To maintain listener interest it combines neume motifs, harmonic sequences, Middle Eastern diatonicism, motivic sequences, operatic cadenzas, register shifts, and a folk refrain. Unfortunately, Rosenblatt never recorded this piece, to which he surely would have brought the same beautiful tone and agile delivery exhibited in the 122 other compositions that he did record.

Hashkiveinu adonai eloheinu,
leshalom . . .

'Cause us, O God, to lie down in peace,
and raise us up, O our King, to life . . .
Shield us from every enemy . . .
Shelter us beneath thy wings . . .
Spread over us thy tabernacle of peace'.

EXAMPLE 8.4
"Golden Age" set piece, published by Yossele Rosenblatt.

Between the World Wars

The 1932 *Union Hymnal*, while including new settings by European refugees Joseph Achron (1886–1943), Heinrich Schalit (1886–1976), and Jacob Weinberg (1879–1956), also quotes Mozart (hymn #10), Haydn (hymn #60), Rossini (hymn #140), and Handel (hymn #175).

The 1933 *Sacred Service* of Ernest Bloch (1880–1959), commissioned by a Reform Group in San Francisco, is a high-water mark of 20th-century Synagogue song. EXAMPLE 8.5[11] shows the seventh part of Kedushah.

> *Echad hu eloheinu . . .*
> 'One is our God, our Father, our Saviour;
> and He in his mercy will again proclaim to us,
> in the presence of all living' . . .

From *Sacred Service* by Ernest Bloch. Copyright © 1934 by Summy-Birchard Publishing Company. Renewal, 1962, assigned to Broude Brothers. Copyright © 1962 by Broude Brothers. Reprinted by permission of the publisher.

EXAMPLE 8.5
Development of a melody reminiscent of a *Misinai* Tune: from Bloch's *Sacred Service.*

Cantor and choir alternate in developing a melody reminiscent of *Misinai* Tune 22 (see Appendix C, left-hand column). Be it coincidence or the unconscious recapturing of a traditional melody heard in childhood, the fact is that Bloch succeeded in evoking something from deep within Synagogal tradition. He treated the elusive strain as only a composer familiar with chazanic practice could: responsively. Not since Salomon Sulzer's mid-19th century Vienna heyday had cantorial statements interacted so organically with choral commentary.

In addition to Bloch, composers Lazare Saminsky (1882–1959), Frederick Jacobi (1891–1952), Abraham Binder (1895–1967), and Lazar Weiner (1897–1982) also helped reshape the Reform service, choosing thematic material from Biblical chant. We know this was their intent from their own testimony in the form of lectures, essays, and introductions to the liturgical collections in which the following four excerpts appeared.

EXAMPLE 8.6a,[12] by Saminsky, is from the conclusion of every Amidah:

> May the words of my mouth
> and the meditations of my heart
> be acceptable unto thee, O Lord,
> my Rock and my Redeemer, amen.

EXAMPLE 8.6b,[13] by Jacobi, is from the second blessing preceding the evening Shema, *Ahavat Olam* ('With Everlasting Love'):

> *nasi'ach bechukecha . . .*
> 'we rejoice in thy laws'.

EXAMPLE 8.6c,[14] by Binder, is from the Shofar ritual according to Reform usage, that portion of the Rosh Hashanah liturgy in which a ram's horn is sounded to announce God's Kingship over the nations.

> The Lord reigneth (Psalm 47:8).

EXAMPLE 8.6d,[15] by Weiner, is from *Lechah, Dodi* ('Come, My Beloved'), a *Kabbalat Shabbat* hymn introduced by the mystics of Safed in the Galilee, during the 16th century.

Sof ma'aseh bemachashavah techilah . . .
'Sabbath was first in God's scheme, but the
last to be wrought'.

Neume-motif parallels to the right of each of the above four musical
illustrations follow Solomon Rosowsky's codification of the Lithuanian
Biblical-chant tradition (see Appendix B).[16]

EXAMPLE 8.6
Biblically-inspired Reform settings.

Among mid-20th century Orthodox cantors of repute were: Benzion
Kapov-Kagan (1899–1953); Moishe Oysher (1907–1958); Leibele
Waldman (1907–1969); and Moshe Ganchoff (1905–). Their recordings
attest to an accomplished vocalism devoted more to rehashing the prior
generation's proven formulas than to serious attempts at originality.
Conservative cantors followed Orthodox practice except that they
avoided the improvisation crucial to Orthodox style.

Post World-War II

As a result of the decimation of European Jewry during World War II, American Synagogue song was finally on its own. Joining Eastern European immigrants Moshe Koussevitsky (1899–1966), Israel Alter (1901–1979), Jacob Koussevitsky (1903–1959), David Koussevitsky (1911–1979), and Sholom Katz (1919–1982), were two native American cantors, Jan Peerce (1904–1984), and Richard Tucker (1914–1975). With European *chazanut* in decline, the Reform, Conservative, and Orthodox movements launched American cantorial schools, including the School of Sacred Music (1948); the Cantors Institute (1952); and the Cantorial Training Institute (1954). Their alumni graduated into professional cantorial organizations of the three movements: Cantors Assembly (Conservative, 1947); American Conference of Certified Cantors (Reform, 1953); and Cantorial Council (Orthodox, 1960).

In 1954 the School of Sacred Music reissued 25 *Out of Print Classics of Synagogue Music*, documenting continuity in 19th-century European practice. Volume Six, for instance, a 1905 edition of 1839 material from Vienna, offers the Call to Prayer, *Barechu*, from Friday Night Maariv in "plagal" major *Adonai Malach* (EXAMPLE 8.7a).[17] Volume 24, from Czestochowa, Poland, 1908, does likewise (EXAMPLE 8.7b).[18]

Cantor's call: *Barechu et adonai hamevorach . . .*
'Bless ye the Lord who is to be praised';

Congregation's response: *baruch adonai hamvorach le'olam va'ed*
'blessed is the Lord who is to be praised forevermore'.

Compare *Barechu* Examples 8.7a and 8.7b with the opening line of *Hashkiveinu*, Example 6.8b.

Eastern European immigrants to America modified this Friday Night Maariv tradition, preferring a "plagal" minor mode. The shift to minor—in the congregation's response—surfaced in 1951 (EXAMPLE 8.7c).[19] Compare the 8.5c congregation's response to the Friday Night Maariv Closing-blessing motif of Example 7.8c, in the "plagal"-minor mode of Selichah-*Techinah*.

By 1968 the transition to "plagal"-minor Selichah-*Techinah* was complete (EXAMPLE 8.7d);[20] American Jewry preferred this Prayer mode until very recently. EXAMPLE 8.7e[21] shows two parallels to American Friday Night practice, in Kol Nidre, sung as the *Techinah*-section of a three-part Selichah mode. The two Kol Nidre motifs, paralleling *et adonai* ('the Lord') and *hamvorach* ('who is to be praised'), bracketed in Friday Night Example 8.7d, use *Misinai* Tunes 39 and 14 , charted as part of the Selichah-*Techinah* mode in Example 6.10b).

EXAMPLE 8.7

Progression of mode for Friday Night Maariv: "plagal" major to plagal" minor; parallel in Selichah-*Techinah*.

An "authentic" minor mode, *Magein Avot*, for chanting Hallel, typifies the Conservative approach to Synagogue song of a generation ago. EXAMPLE 8.8a,[22] composer unknown, quotes music from the lovers' Betrothal Duet, "Ot, Der Brunem" ('There, The Well'), from the 1880 Biblical Yiddish operetta, *Shulamis* (EXAMPLE 8.6b).[23]

> *Lo Hameitim yehalelu yah . . .*
> 'The dead do not praise the Lord,
> nor do any that go down into silence'
> (Psalm 115:17).

The operetta's composer, Abraham Goldfaden (1840–1908), in turn, paraphrased Violetta's aria, "Ah, fors'è lui ('Ah, Perhaps He Is The One'), from Verdi's *La Traviata* (1853; EXAMPLE 8.8c).[24]

EXAMPLE 8.8
"Authentic"-minor *Magein Avot* mode in Hallel; its derivation from Yiddish operetta and Italian opera.

Post–Vietnam

Within the past 20 years American congregations have attempted to recapture the fervor of traditional prayer. In 1968 a semi-staged review of Chasidic tales—*Ish Chasid Hayah* ('Once There Was A Chasid')—interspersed with *nigunim* (melodies without words), so fired the imagination of its Tel Aviv audience that an annual Chasidic Song Festival ensued. Winning entries swept American Jewish communities through recordings, sheet music, and touring troupes.

Chasidic-style tunes borrowed liturgical texts like the final strophe of the Amidah for every service,

> *Oseh shalom bimromav . . .*
> 'He who makes peace in the heavens, grant
> peace to us and unto all Israel, and let us say,
> amen'.

At first, the tunes were in "authentic" minor (EXAMPLE 8.9a).[25] A later version of the same text shifted to "plagal" minor (EXAMPLE 8.9b).[26] The American trend toward "plagal"-minor Chasidic-style prayer—documented in Friday Night practice (Example 8.7)—has continued in this country with the concluding Kedushah-refrain:

> *Ledor vador nagid godlecha . . .*
> 'All generations recount thy greatness'
> (EXAMPLE 8.9c).[27]

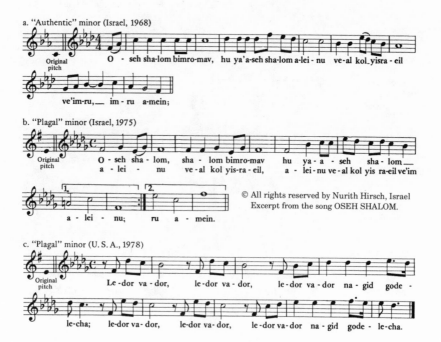

EXAMPLE 8.9
Chasidic-style tunes in "authentic"-minor and "plagal"-minor modes.

Of late, guitar-playing Reform cantors are *de rigeur*, and informal dress and demeanor have entered Conservative Judaism through the Havurah ('Fellowship') Movement. Amateur groups have deposed professional choirs in some Reform congregations, while choral music of any kind is fast disappearing from Conservative and Orthodox synagogues.

In all three movements of American Judaism, unison congregational singing is the norm, bypassing *davenen*, an untranslatable term connoting the historically lively give-and-take between cantor and congregation. That cherished repository of prescribed figurations—Biblical chant—is frequently mishandled by lay readers. Responsive readings are interspersed with Neo-Chasidic *nigunim*, often accompanied by handclapping.

Influence of American Folk and Popular Music

One by one, the European-born cantors who carried on their Synagogal tradition amid the strange surroundings of a secular America, are retiring from the scene. The baton is now passing to a younger generation of American-born cantors, men and women, preoccupied with survival in a nuclear age. They were raised to believe in the American Way of Life, "the operative faith of the American people," as Will Herberg puts it.[28] Based on democratic ideals (Life, Liberty, the Pursuit of Happiness), boasting saints (Washington and Lincoln), symbols (Stars and Stripes), festivals (Fourth of July), holy writ (Constitution and Bill of Rights), and songs (Rock and Roll), the American Way of Life summarizes our society's drift toward what might be called National Secularism.

The songs particularly pervade America's Nationalist-Secularist existence, influencing attitudes and behavior. Contemporary songwriters—including synagogue cantors—have had to look no farther than American folk song for music expressive of the American Way of Life. One melodic/cadential pattern is so common that I call it the "American-Way-of-Life" motif. Neume-like, its absolute pitches vary according to the occasion and type of song, yet it is always recognizable: optimistic and sure of itself.

EXAMPLE 8.10 cites the motif in nine songs[29] that span almost a century-and-a-half (1845–1981). They cover the gamut of American life: Children (EXAMPLE 8.10a); Patriotism (EXAMPLE 8.10b); Work (EXAMPLE 8.10c); Leisure (EXAMPLE 8.10d); Winter Holiday (EXAMPLE

EXAMPLE 8.10
The American-Way-of-Life motif 1845–1981.

8.10e); Hymn (EXAMPLE 8.10f); Spiritual (EXAMPLE 8.10g); Peace
(EXAMPLE 8.10h); and Love (EXAMPLE 8.10i). All the songs appear in
D "authentic" major to facilitate comparison; the motif itself describes a
descent from $\underline{A}$ to $\underline{D}$, with $\underline{B}$, $\underline{G}$, $\underline{F}^\sharp$, and $\underline{E}$ serving as passing tones.

Synagogue cantors of the 1980s are fusing recent folk and popular practices because their musical formulas echo American Jewry's current Rock-and-Roll environment. Borrowing the American-Way-of-Life motif observed in Example 8.10, contemporary cantors have applied it to lyrics[30] that talk of Peace (EXAMPLE 8.11a) and related concerns like Ecology (EXAMPLE 8.11b) and Life (EXAMPLE 8.11c).

> *8.11a — Shalom rav al yisra'eil amcha . . .*
> 'Grant lasting peace to thy people, Israel';

> *8.11b — Vayar elohim . . .*
> 'And God saw all his work, and it was good';

> *8.11c — Lechayim, velo . . .*
> 'May God renew this month for Life'.

Phrased in a rock-rhythm, the 8.11 Examples 'push the beat', i.e., sing an eighth-note ahead of time and tie it to the following note on which the actual beat occurs. Thus an iambic prayer-text like *Shalom Rav* (EXAMPLE 8.11d) is made to resemble colloquial speech (EXAMPLE 8.11e).These kinds of rhythms and stresses, reminiscent of 'Black English' (EXAMPLE 8.11f, same as Example 8.10c), have pervaded American popular music for over a century. Synagogue song is following suit; in short, it is being Americanized.

EXAMPLE 8.11
The American-Way-of-Life motif in Synagogue song 1981–1986.

Ironically, the American-Way-of-Life motif used in the Synagogue melodies of Example 8.11 is similar to the "authentic"-major pattern of worship shared by every diaspora community, the universal *Tefillah* ('Prayer') mode, *Adonai Malach.* (Refer to **PART III, CHAPTER FIVE**: Notes 16 through 24). Secure in its freedom, American Jewry is now choosing praise over petition. (See **PART II, CHAPTER THREE, Misinai Tunes: Occurrences**). Increasingly, prayers are sung in Laudatory *Adonai Malach* rather than in Penitential Selichah-*Techinah* (see **PART III, CHAPTER SIX**, Examples 6.13 and 6.14).

EXAMPLE 8.12a[31] shows opening and closing motifs [1] and [4] of the *Adonai Malach* mode. *Adonai Malach* motifs [1] and [4], in turn, parallel *Misinai* Tunes ⬚1 and ⬚17 (see Example 5.3e and Appendix C).

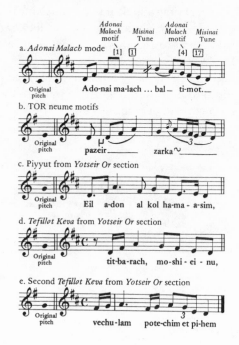

Adonai malach . . . / / . . . bal timot
'The Lord reigns [robed in majesty] . . . / /
[The world] shall never be moved'.

EXAMPLE 8.12
Adonai Malach parallels with the American-Way-of-Life motif.

TOR neume-motif equivalents for Adonai Malach motifs [1] and [4] appear in EXAMPLE 8.12b.[32]

Such widespread usage of the Laudatory mode finds precedent in the 19th-century Shabbat Shacharit practice of many European Ashkenazic communities, East and West. EXAMPLE 8.12c,[33] a Piyyut; EXAMPLES 8.12d[34] and 8.12e,[35] both *Tefillot Keva*, all portray the heavenly hosts' echoing of God's praise in the *Yotseir Or* ('Creator of Light') section which heralds the morning Shema and Amidah, thus anchoring the Statutory prayers of Shacharit.

> 8.12c — *Eil adon al kol hama'asim . . .*

'God, the Lord over all creation';

> 8.12d — *titbarach, moshi'einu . . .*

'Be thou blessed, our Redeemer';

> 8.12e — *vechulam potechim et pihem . . .*

'The angels declare God's holiness'.

All of this helps to explain the recent blending of Ashkenazic tradition with American environmental influence. Even Orthodoxy does not escape the Americanization process. Our final musical Example offers an Orthodox setting of a liturgical text. This type of setting was popularized as a *Ruach* (sing-along) song for-all-occasions during the 1970s. Although Orthodoxy prefers to elevate derivative material from the realm of 'profane' to that of 'sacred', it too has lately opted for "authentic"-major *Adonai Malach*-style melodies. EXAMPLE 8.13,[36] *Achas Sho'alti* ('One thing have I asked of the Lord'; Psalm 27:4), echoes the American-Way-of-Life motif, but in four-square rhythm.

> . . . *kol yemei chayai*
> '[that I may dwell in the
> house of the Lord]
> all the days of my life'.

EXAMPLE 8.13
American influence on an Orthodox *Ruach*-song of the 1970s.

Conclusion: A Mixed Offering

Does the foregoing spell salvation for American Synagogue song in the 21st century? The question is better phrased: How much host-culture influence is too much? To answer it we refer back to the motto with which this book began,

> I raise my hands . . . with offer mixed.

To be acceptable, I believe that the *Mixed Offering* of American cantors should represent all segments of an American Jewry still unpacking the cultural baggage of its many earlier host countries. That baggage includes: Sephardic hymns (Example 8.1); Viennese waltzes and Parisian-operetta melodies (Example 8.2); German call-and-response hymns (Example 8.3); cantorial recitatives, unaccompanied or with choral commentary (Examples 8.4, 8.5); Italian-opera airs and Yiddish-theater duets (Example 8.8); American-Way-of-Life-inspired anthems which coincide with the Universal Prayer mode, *Adonai Malach* (Example 8.12); and *Ruach*-songs for-all-occasions (Example 8.13).

Like the Temple offering of old, our Synagogue offering is a mixture. Once its ingredients are thoroughly blended, the offering yields "a pleasing odor to the Lord" (Leviticus 2:9):

> When anyone brings . . . a mixed offering to
> the Lord, it shall be of fine flour; he shall
> pour oil upon it, and put frankincense on it
> (Leviticus 2:1).

Mixed Offering in Hebrew is *Minchat Arev*, the word *arev* allowing three different meanings: 'mixture'; 'sweet'; or 'evening'. After three centuries, American Synagogue song is just beginning to blend. Time will tell whether it will be well-mixed and hence sweet-smelling, or merely a prolonged Evensong

> whose time is fixed.

The Americanization of Synagogue Song: A Survey: Bibliography & Notes

1. LEVY, Isaac: *Antología de Liturgia Judeo-Española*, Jerusalem, Ministry of Education and Culture (1975), Volume VII, pages 21–22.
2. AGUILAR, Emanuel, David Aaron de Sola, and E.R.Jessurun: *Sephardi Melodies*, London, Oxford (1931), page 30.
3. DAVIS, Moshe: *The Emergence of Conservative Judaism*, Philadelphia, Jewish Publication Society (1963), pages 6–8.
4. WISE, Isaac Mayer: *Reminiscences* (Cincinnati, 1901) translated from the German by David Philipson, New York, Central Synagogue (1945), page 45; Wise recalled the typical mid-19th century American cantor as being "half priest, half beggar, half oracle, half fool, as the occasion demanded." An intermittent 1857 correspondence between the editor of *The Occident and American Jewish Advocate*, Isaac Leeser, and an anonymous reader, bears out Wise's recollection.
5. SULZER, Salomon: *Schir Zion*, Vienna, published by the author (1839), number 18.
6. NAUMBOURG, Samuel: *Chants religieux des Israëlites*, Paris, published by the author (1847), number 42.
7. ARENSBERG, Conrad: "American Communities," (*American Anthropologist*, 1955), reprinted in *Readings in Anthropology*, edited by Morton H. Fried, New York, Crowell (1959), Volume II, page 361.
8. LEWANDOWSKY, Louis: *Todah W'simrah*, Berlin, published by the author (1876), number 83.
9. PHONOGRAPH RECORDINGS: For this telling analysis I am indebted to Henry Sapoznik, Curator of the Cantorial-recording Collection at YIVO, New York, private communication (November, 1985).
10. ROSENBLATT, Yossele: *Tefiloth Josef*, New York, Metro (1927), number 4.
11. BLOCH, Ernest: *Avodah Hakodesh*, Boston, Birchard (1934), pages 28–29.
12. SAMINSKY, Lazare: *Sabbath Evening Service*, New York, Bloch (1930), pages 26–27.
13. JACOBI, Frederick: *Ahavas Olom*, New York, Bloch (1952), page 7.
14. BINDER, Abraham W.: *Morning Service for the New Year*, New York, Transcontinental (1957), page 38.
15. WEINER, Lazar: *Likras Shabos*, New York, Mills (1954), page 3.
16. ROSOWSKY, Solomon: *Neume Motifs for the Yearly Cycle of Biblical Chant, According to the Lithuanian Tradition*, after manuscripts, New York, Jewish Theological Seminary (1958); Appendix B.
17. SULZER (see item 5), number 20; number 25 in 1905 revision.
18. BIRNBAUM, Abraham Ber: *Amanut Hachazanut*, Czestochaw, published by the author (1908), number 30.
19. IDELSOHN, Abraham Zvi: *The Jewish Song Book*, edited by Baruch Cohon, Cincinnati, Publications for Judaism (1951), page 17.

20. ALTER, Israel: *The Sabbath Service*, New York, Cantors Assembly (1968), pages 11–12.

21. OGUTSCH, Fabian: *Der Frankfurter Kantor*, Frankfurt, Israelitischen Gemeinde (1930), number 23.

22. HALLEL: *Festival Kit*, compiled and edited by Max Wohlberg, New York, Jewish Theological Seminary (circa 1950).

23. GOLDFADEN, Abraham: *Shulamis*, New York, Hebrew Publishing (1912), number 9.

24. VERDI, Giuseppe: "La Traviata," *Seven Verdi Librettos,* edited by William Weaver, New York, Norton (1975), page 185.

25. HIRSCH, Nurit: "Oseh Shalom," *Hassidic Song Festival,* Tel Aviv, Hed Arzi recording BAN 1421 (1968), side 2, band 1.; transcribed by Joseph A. Levine.

26. SIROTKIN, Reuven: *Hassidic Festival Songbook*, Tel Aviv (1975), page 18.

27. ZIM, Sol: *The Joy of Shabbos Songbook*, New York, Tara (1978), page 52.

28. HERBERG, Will: *Protestant, Catholic, Jew*, Garden City, Doubleday (1960), pages 74–88.

29. a.OBERNDORFER, Anne & Max: *New American Song Book*, 1941, page 120 ("Polly Wolly Doodle");

b. MADDY, Joseph E. & W. Otto Miessner: *All-American Song Book*, 1942, page 30 ("Marines' Hymn");

c. WORK, John W.: *American Negro Songs and Spirituals*, (1940, page 37 ("O, Captain");

d.BONI, Margaret Bradford: *Fireside Book of Folk Songs*, 1947, page 102 ("Halelujah, I'm a Bum");

e. WELLS, Katharine Tyler: *Golden Song Book*, 1945, page 73 ("Jingle Bells");

f. BONI (see item 29d), page 282 ("My Faith Looks Up To Thee");

g. WORK (see item 29c), page 66 ("Ain't You Glad");

h. SEEGER, Pete: "Where Have All The Flowers Gone?" in *Great Songs of the Sixties,* edited by Milton Okun, New York, Random House (1961), page 310;

i. BACHRACH, Burt: "Best That You Can Do," in *Song Classics of the '80s,* New York, Warner Brothers (1982), page 2.

30. a. KLEPPER, Jeff & Daniel Freelander: "Shalom Rav," in *Shiron Leshalom*, North American Federation of Temple Youth (1981), page 22;

b. LUSTIG, Gordon: "Hineh Tov Me'od," in *A Sourcebook of Jewish Songs for Peace*, Jewish Educators for Social Responsibility (1986), page 10;

c. SCHILLER, Steven: "Livrachah," in *Shiron Leshalom* (see item 30a), page 28.

31. IDELSOHN, Abraham Zvi: "The Traditional Song of the South German Jews," *Thesaurus of Hebrew Oriental Melodies*, Leipzig, Hofmeister (1933), Volume VII, page xx.

32. SULZER, (see item 5), 1905 reissue, number 108, neume motif 14 (TOR).

33. SULZER (see item 5), 1905 reissue, number 64.

34. LEWANDOWSKY, LOUIS: *Kol Rinnah U't'fillah*, Berlin, published by the author (1871), number 32.

35. GLANTZ, Leib: *Rinat Hakodesh*, Tel Aviv, Israel Music Institute (1968), page 69.

36. MERNICK, S.: "Achas Sho-alti," in *Hassidic-Style Hits of the '70s*, edited by Velvel Pasternak, New York, Tara (1975), page 9.

PART V

WORKING APPENDICES

Appendix A reviews Hebrew and technical terms that have appeared in the book. Appendices B and C will help the reader verify sources of motifs within published material, or discover ways to enrich his or her own style of sacred chant.

Appendix A - GLOSSARY

Adonai Malach ('The Lord Reigns'). Laudatory Principal Prayer mode similar to Arabic *Makam Siga*; major-sounding mode featuring lowered seventh and tenth degrees in its upper octave.

Ahavah Rabah ('With Abounding Love'). Supplicatory Principal Prayer mode similar to Arabic *Makam Hijaz*.

Aleinu ('Adoration'). Sung to *Misinai* Tunes during HHD Musaf Amidah, within prescribed modes or freely at all other times (Example 3.11, Prayer-type 1.e; Appendix C, $\boxed{11}$, $\boxed{12}$).

A Lith. American-Lithuanian tradition of Biblical chant, an offshoot of Eastern Ashkenazic practice.

Amidah ('Standing Devotion'). The backbone of every service.

Anshei Ma'amad ('Standing Delegates'). Groups attending Second Temple rites in Jerusalem semi-annually, from Judea's 24 provinces.

Ash. Ashkenazic (Northern European) tradition of Biblical chant, including German (Western) and Lithuanian (Eastern) subdivisions and offshoots such as English (German) and Jerusalem (Lithuanian).

"authentic" mode. Concentrates its motifs characteristically from the tonic to an octave above.

Avot ('Patriarchal Prayer'). Sung to *Misinai* Tunes during HHD Schacharit, Musaf, and Minchah, within prescribed modes or freely at other times (Example 3.11, Prayer-type 1.c; Appendix C, $\boxed{7}$).

azlá ('going on'). Additional separator neume; column 8.a in Appendix B.

Bab. Babylonian tradition of Biblical chant, an offshoot of Oriental Jewry's Middle Eastern subdivision.

Balt. Baltimore tradition of Biblical chant, a combination of German and Lithuanian Ashkenazic practice.

Barechu ('Call to Prayer'). Sung to *Misinai* Tunes during HHD and FEST Maariv, within prescribed modes or freely at other times (Example 3.11, Prayer-type 1.a; Appendix C, $\boxed{1}$, $\boxed{2}$, $\boxed{3}$, $\boxed{4}$).

cantillation (from Latin *cantillare*, 'sing low'). Since the 18th century, the term applied to: a) Biblical chant; b) patterned recitation of any text.

Chasidic ('pious'). Devout Jewish sect which considers song the epitome of prayer.

chazanut. The art of a cantor (*chazan*).

chazanut haregesh ('Dionysian'). Emotional, free-wheeling cantorial singing.

chazanut haseider ('Apollonian'). Formal, planned cantorial singing.

chefulah ('double lengthening'). Substitute neume for *tevir*; column 6.d in Appendix B.

coloratura. Melismatic flourishes.

Congregational Egalitarianism. Late-17th to early-18th century American system which saw each isolated community set its own religious standards without hierarchical interference.

connectors. Seven neumes whose motifs and the motif of the following neume should be sung without pause: *mercha   munach mahpach darga   ketanah^{Q} kadma   yerach-ben-yomo*.

darga ('step'). Connector neume; column 6.a in Appendix B.

davenen. Yiddish for: a) pray; b) give-and-take between cantor and congregation.

E Seph. Eastern subdivision of Sephardic tradition of Biblical chant, centering in the Balkans.

Eng. English tradition of Biblical chant, an offshoot of the German subdivision of Ashkenazic practice.

EST. Book of Esther, read on Purim, late-winter festival commemorating Israel's deliverance from genocide in ancient Persia.

ethos. A mode's characteristic mood (after Aristotle: *Metaphysics* 8.5).

etnachta ('rest'). Chief separator neume of Etnachta group; column 2.d in Appendix B.

F Seph. French Sephardic tradition of Biblical chant, an offshoot of Western Sephardic practice.

FEST ('Pilgrimage Festivals'). Pesach, Shavuot, and Sukkot, observed in: early spring; early summer; and early autumn.

gadòl ('large rise'). Substitute neume for katon; column 4.e in Appendix B.

ᵒgedolah ('large extension'). Additional separator neume; column 8.e in Appendix B.

ʾgeireish ('expulsion'). Additional separator neume; column 8.b in Appendix B.

^Ger. German tradition of Biblical chant, a subdivision of Ashkenazic practice.

gershaꞌyim ('double expulsion'). Additional separator neume; column 8.c in Appendix B.

Golden Section. Proportion much found in art, where the larger part is to the smaller as the sum of the pair is to the larger.

Haggadah. Passover Eve 'telling' of the Israelites' Exodus from Egypt.

Hallel. Psalms of Praise (113-118), sung during FEST Shacharit.

harmonic minor. "Plagal" mode similar to Selichah-*Techinah* Prayer mode in its raised seventh degree, creating a leading tone to the tonic and an augmented-second interval between the sixth and seventh degrees.

Hashkiveinu ('Cause us, our God, to lie down in peace'). Night-prayer whose central portion, *Vehagein ba'adeinu* ('Shield us from enemy, pestilence, sword, famine, and sorrow') is often sung in the Selichah-*Techinah* mode.

HHD. High Holy Days of Rosh Hashanah and Yom Kippur, varying between early-September and mid-October.

Hijaz. Arabic secular mode, similar to *Ahavah Rabah* in its augmented-second interval between the second and third degrees.

Hijaz-Kar. Arabic secular mode of the *Hijaz*-type, featuring an additional augmented-second interval between its sixth and seventh degrees.

Industrial-age Elitism. Two-tiered 19th-century social structure wherein factory-owner Church trustees imported well-known ministers who preached to worker-parishioners.

Introit ('entry'). Introductory passage to a liturgical section.

^Jer. Jerusalem tradition of Biblical chant, offshoot of Lithuanian subdivision of Ashkenazic practice.

JUB. Jubilatory treatment of a neume group in certain dramatic passages of Biblical chant.

Kabbalat Shabbat ('Sabbath Welcome'). Friday Night sundown service.

Kaddish ('Doxology'). Sung to *Misinai* Tunes during HHD and FEST; to traditional melodies, within prescribed modes, or freely at other times (Example 3.11, Prayer-type 1.f; Appendix C, 13 , 14).

kadmá ('preceding'). Additional connector neume; column 7.d in Appendix B.

ᵖ*karnei-farah*ᵠ ('heifer's horns'). Additional separator neume; column 8.g in Appendix B.

katón ('small rise'). Chief separator neume of Katon group; column 4.d in Appendix B.

Kedushah ('Sanctification'). Sung to *Misinai* Tunes during HHD Shacharit, Musaf, Minchah, and Neilah; freely at other times (Example 3.11, Prayer-type 1.d; Appendix C, 8 , 9 , 10).

*ketanah*ᵠ ('small extension'). Additional connector neume; column 7.c in Appendix B.

Kol Nidre ('All Vows'). Thousand-year-old Aramaic formula annulling all personal pledges to God; considered the classic middle, or *Techinah* ('Pleading')-section of the three-part Selichah mode, its melody includes more *Misinai* Tunes than that of any other prayer.

LAM. Book of Lamentations, read on Tishah B'av (Ninth of Av) mid-summer fast mourning the sack of both Temples.

legarmeh| ('by itself'). Separator neume; column 5.a in Appendix B.

leinen ('to read'). Yiddish for Biblical chant.

Lishkat Hagazit ('Chamber of Hewn Stone'). Seat of the Great Sanhedrin, or High Court of Justice; also served as synagogue in the Second Temple.

ᴸⁱᵗʰ. Lithuanian tradition of Biblical chant, Eastern subdivision of Ashkenazic practice.

Maariv. Ashkenazic name for Evening service (Arvit in Sephardic usage).

Magein ('Concerning "Shield of Abraham" '). Sung to *Misinai* Tunes during HHD, FEST, and SAB Shacharit, plus Minchah and Neilah on Yom Kippur (Example 3.11, Prayer-type II.k; Appendix C, 23).

Magein Avot ('Our Forbears' Shield'). Didactic Principal Prayer mode similar to Arabic secular modes: Bayat (stressing D̲) and Bayat-Nava (stressing G̲).

mahpach ('reversed'). Connector neume; column 4.a in Appendix B.

makam. Arabic secular mode (plural, *makamat*).

Malchuyot ('Kingship Verses'). First of three sections inserted in Rosh Hashanah Musaf Amidah.

Mechayeh ('Concerning "Resurrection" '). Sung to *Misinai* Tunes during HHD, FEST, and SAB Shacharit, plus Minchah and Neilah on Yom Kippur (Example 3.11, Prayer-type II.1; Appendix C, 24 , 25).

Megillot (singular, *Megillah*). Scrolls of EST, RES, LAM, read on Purim, Pilgrimage Festivals, and Tishah B'av.

melismatic tone density. Unlimited number of notes per syllable.

Me'orah ('Concerning "The Creator of Light" '). Sung to *Misinai* Tunes during HHD, FEST, and SAB Shacharit (Example 3.11, Prayer-type I.g; Appendix C, 16 , 17 , 18).

mercha ('lengthening'). Connector neume; columns 1.a and 1.c, 2.a, 6.b, 9.a and 9.c, 10.a and 10.c, 11.a and 11.e and 11.g, 12.a and12.e, in Appendix B.

Meshulash ('Concerning "Tripartite Sanctification" '). Sung to *Misinai* Tunes during HHD, FEST, and SAB Shacharit and Musaf, plus Minchah and Neilah on Yom Kippur (Example 3.11, Prayer-type II.m; Appendix C, 26 , 27).

microtone. Interval smaller than the Western half-tone.

Midrash. Exposition on Jewish theme, either Halachic (legal) or Aggadic (narrative).

Minchah. Afternoon service.

Minhag. A community's liturgical custom.

Minyan. Quorum of 10 adults needed to conduct public worship.

Misinai ('From Mount Sinai') Tunes. Twelfth-century Rhineland Biblical neume motifs, still sung in Ashkenazic Prayer-mode chant; Appendix C lists 39 Primary Occurrences, 67 Recurrences, and 54 Parallels.

motif. Characteristic grouping of as few as two notes.

muezzin. Muslim 'Caller-to-Prayer'.

munach ('resting'). Connector neume; Columns 2.c, 3.a and 3.c, 4.c, 5.b, 7.a, 11.c, and 12.b, in Appendix B.

Musaf. Late-morning ('Additional') service.

National Secularism. Faith in American democracy; in its manner has its own saints, symbols, festivals, holy writ, and songs.

Nechamah ('Consolation'). Closing of Selichah mode, in either "authentic" *Adonai Malach* or *Magein Avot*, identical to opening *Vidui* ('Confessional').

Neilah ('Closing of the Gates'). Concluding Yom Kippur service.

neumatic tone density. Averages two-to-five notes per syllable,typical of Biblical neume motifs.

neume. Symbol indicating relative pitch (and rhythm) of a Biblical-chant motif; *ta'am* in Hebrew, sometimes translated as 'trope'.

Nigun. Wordless Chasidic melody.

nusach ('formula'). Refers primarily to Prayer-rubric, secondarily to chant patterns.

Ofan ('Concerning "Angels" '). Sung to *Misinai* Tunes during HHD, FEST, and SAB Shacharit (Example 3.11, Prayer-type II.h; Appendix C, 19 , 20).

Oriental (non-Occidental). Third main branch of world Jewry (after Ashkenazic and Sephardic); subdivisions are North African and Middle Eastern, offshoots include Moroccan and Syrian.

*pashta*ʼ ('stretcher'). Separator neume; column 4.b in Appendix B.

Pasuk ('Individual Biblical Verse'). Sung to *Misinai* Tunes: on minor fasts during Shacharit and Minchah; in month of Elul during pre-dawn Selichot; on Yom Kippur during Maariv, Shacharit, Musaf, Minchah, and Neilah (Example 3.11, Prayer-type III.o; Appendix C, 29).

payyetanim (singular, *payyetan*). Liturgical poets.

paz̆eir ('dispersed'). Additional separator neume; column 8.d in Appendix B.

pesik | ('stop'). Non-vocalized separator neume; column 5.a in Appendix B.

Pesukei Dezimra ('Passages of Song'). Pre-Shacharit prayers.

piyyutim (from Piyyut, 'poetry'). Laudatory hymns added within sections of Statutory prayer.

"plagal" mode. Concentrates its motifs characteristically from a fourth below the tonic to a fifth above.

Prayer mode. Sacred vocal pattern of traditional motifs that retains its identity even though melody, rhythm, note-intervals, and note-sequences change.

Prayer-types. Example 3.11 catalogues 18 as: I. Statutory Prayers (*Tefillot Keva*); II. Laudatory Poems (*Piyyutim*); amd III. Penitential Laments (*Selichot*).

Psalm Tones. Eight formulas for reciting Psalms during Roman Catholic daily Office, consisting of opening figure, reciting-tone, and closing figure, in each half of verse.

'pushing the beat'. In rock-rhythm, sounding and eighth-note ahead of time and tieing it to the note on which the actual beat occurs.

reciting-tone (≠). Single pitch on which innumerable syllables are intoned.

RES. Ruth-Ecclesiastes-Song of Solomon, read during: Shavuot; Sukkot; and Pesach.

Reshut ('Concerning "Divine Permission" '). Sung to *Misinai* Tunes during HHD, FEST, and SAB Shacharit and Musaf, plus Minchah and Neilah on Yom Kippur (Example 3.11, Prayer-type II.j; Appendix C, 22).

revi'a ('rhomboid'). Chief separator neume of Revi'a group; column 5.c in Appendix B.

SAB. Sabbath (Shabbat in Hebrew).

segol ⁙ ('cluster'). Chief separator neume of Segol group (column 3.d in Appendix B).

Selichah ('Individual Composed Verse'). Sung to *Misinai* Tunes: on minor fasts during Shacharit and Minchah; in month of Elul during pre-dawn Selichot; on Yom Kippur during Maariv, Shacharit, Musaf, Minchah, and Neilah (Example 3.11, Prayer-type III.q; Appendix C, 31, 32).

Selichah (Three-part 'Forgiveness' mode). Consists of: *Vidui* ("authentic" 'Confessional') opening; *Techinah* ("plagal" 'Pleading') middle section ; and *Nechamah* ("authentic" 'Consolation') closing.

Selichah-*Techinah* (Selichah mode's *Techinah* or 'pleading' middle section). "Plagal" harmonic-minor mode based largely on *Misinai* Tunes.

selichot (from *selichah*, 'forgiveness'). Penitential laments added within portions of Statutory prayer.

separators. a) Twelve neumes whose motifs are followed by a pause: *tipcha zarka⁓ pashta⸍ legarmeh | azla geireish gershaʼyim pazeir gedolah ‹ yetiv ᵒkarnei-farah⸰ pesik | ;* b) nine neumes whose motifs are followed by a full stop: *sof-pasuk ⫶ etnachta segol⁚ shalshelet katon gadol revi'a tevir chefulah.*

Seph. Sephardic (Southern European) tradition of Biblical chant, including Western and Eastern subdivisions and many offshoots such as London (Western) and Balkan (Eastern).

Shacharit. Morning service.

shalshelet ('chain'). Substitute neume for *segol*⁚; column 3.e, Appendix B.

shamash. Synagogue sexton who traditionally reads Scripture.

Shema ('Declaration of Faith'). Sung to *Misinai* Tunes during HHD Maariv, Shacharit, and Neilah, freely at other times (Example 3.11, Prayer-type I.b; Appendix C, 5 , 6).

Shofar service. Section of Rosh Hashanah Torah service during which the ram's horn is sounded.

Shofarot ('Revelation Verses'). Last of three sections inserted in Rosh Hashanah Musaf Amidah.

Siddur Tefillah ('Order of Prayer'). Technical name for prayer book; commonly shortened to Siddur.

Sidrei Pesukim ('Grouped Biblical Verses'). Sung to *Misinai* Tunes: on minor fasts during Shacharit and Minchah; in month of Elul during pre-dawn Selichot; on Yom Kippur during Maariv, Shacharit, Musaf, Minchah, and Neilah (Example 3.11, Prayer-type III.r; Appendix C,$\boxed{30}$.

Sidrei Selichot ('Grouped Composed Verses'). Sung to *Misinai* Tunes: on minor fasts during Shacharit and Minchah; in month of Elul during pre-dawn Selichot; on Yom Kippur during Maariv, Shacharit, Musaf, Minchah, and Neilah (Example 3.11, Prayer-type III.r; Appendix C, $\boxed{33}$, $\boxed{34}$, $\boxed{35}$, $\boxed{36}$, $\boxed{37}$, $\boxed{38}$, $\boxed{39}$).

Siluk ('Concerning "Heavenly Ascent" '). Sung to *Misinai* Tunes during HHD, FEST, and SAB Shacharit and Musaf, plus Minchah and Neilah on Yom Kippur (Example 3.11, Prayer-type II.n; Appendix C, $\boxed{28}$).

sof-pasuk⦂ ('verse-end'). Chief separator neume of Sof-pasuk group; columns 1.d, 9.d, 10.d, 11.h, and 12.g, in Appendix B.

Study mode. Secondary Prayer mode whose motifs—built on leaps of octaves, fifths, fourths, and thirds—appear within other modes.

syllabic tone density. One note per syllable.

Talmud. Collective term for Hebrew Mishnah (–200 to 200); Aramaic Gemara (200 to 500), in Jerusalem and Babylonian versions. Additional collections of attributed statements from Mishnaic period are Baraita and Tosefta.

tartil. Arabic non-metrical recitative (*Zogachts* in Yiddish).

te'amim (from *ta'am*: 'taste'; 'accent'; 'sense'). Biblical neumes, sometimes called tropes.

Tefillot Keva. Statutory prayers that recur in every service, formulated by *Anshei Keneset Hagedolah* ('Men of the Great Assembly') between –500 and –200.

Temple. 'First', built by Solomon in –950, razed by Nebuchadnezzar in –586; 'Second', built by Ezra and Nehemiah in –516, destroyed by Titus in 70.

tevir ('broken'). Chief separator neume of Tevir group; column 6.c in Appendix B.

tipcha ('hand'-breadth'). Separator neume; columns 1.b, 2.b, 9.b, 10.b, 11.b and 11.f, 12.a and 12.d, in Appendix B.

tone density. Average number of notes per syllable.

TOR. Torah, the first five books of the Bible. Read during Monday, Thursday, and SAB Shacharit; also during SAB and HHD Minchah (TOR reading during HHD Shacharit employs different neume motifs).

tropes (after Greek *tropos*, 'turn'). Term sometimes used for Biblical neumes or *te'amim*; more commonly: inserting a new text or melody within a traditional Gregorian chant.

Ukranian-Dorian. Minor-sounding Secondary Prayer mode whose motifs characteristically descend within other modes, featuring raised fourth and sixth degrees.

Vidui ('Confessional'). Opening of three-part Selichah mode, in either "authentic" *Adonai Malach* or *Magein Avot,* identical to *Nechamah* ('Consolation') closing.

Vienna *Ritus* (Latin:'rite'). Well-ordered yet emotionally-charged cantorial singing rich in traditional motifs.

^W Seph. Western Sephardic tradition of Biblical chant, subdivision of Sephardic practice, with many offshoots (such as London).

yerach-ben-yomo ('day-old moon'). Additional separator neume; column 7.b in Appendix B.

‹*yetiv* ('staying'). Additional separator neume; column 8.f in Appendix B.

Yotseir Or ('Creator of Light'). First of two blessings ushering in the morning Shema.

zarka ~ ('scatterer'). Separator neume; column 3.c in Appendix B.

zemirah (plural *zemirot*). Sabbath table song.

Zichronot ('Remembrance Verses'). Middle of three sections inserted in Rosh Hashanah Musaf Amidah.

zogachts. Yiddish non-metrical recitative (*tartil* in Arabic).

APPENDIX B

Appendix B offers neume motifs according to the Lithuanian tradition (^{Lith}) for the yearly cycle of Biblical chant. Readings for six different occasions are given as follows:

- I. TOR = Weekday: Torah (Pentateuch)
- II. HAF = Weekday: Haftarah (Prophets)
- III. HHD = High Holy Day: Torah
- IV. RES = Festival: Ruth-Ecclesiastes-Song of Solomon
- V. LAM = Tishah B'av: Lamentations
- VI. EST = Purim: Esther

Appendix B reads left-to-right, horizontally. It follows Solomon Rosowsky's division of the 28 neumes (graphic symbols of the motifs) into six basic groups (see Example 3.4 in main text of book):

1. Sof-pasuk
2. Etnachta
3. Segol
4. Katon
5. Revi'a
6. Tevir

The motifs for each neume group are charted as columns 1–6. The remaining columns include:

7. Additional-connector motifs
8. Additional-separator motifs
9. Special motifs for Sof-pasuk group at conclusion of chapter/portion
10. Special motifs for Sof-pasuk group at conclusion of book

In Category 9., line V LAM, the third chapter is read according to the (a)-(b)-(c) sequence, without a special conclusion. Category 11., Motifs for Song at the Sea (Exodus 15:1-21), and Category 12., Motifs for Days of Creation (Genesis 1:1-31), both occur twice yearly. Song-at-the-Sea motifs [11.] also serve for the Israelites' wanderings in the wilderness (Numbers 33:1-49).

APPENDIX B

Appendix B. Neume motifs for the yearly cycle of Biblical chant according to the Lithuanian tradition: Solomon Rosowsky (1958)

7. Additional-connector motifs

8. Additional-separator motifs

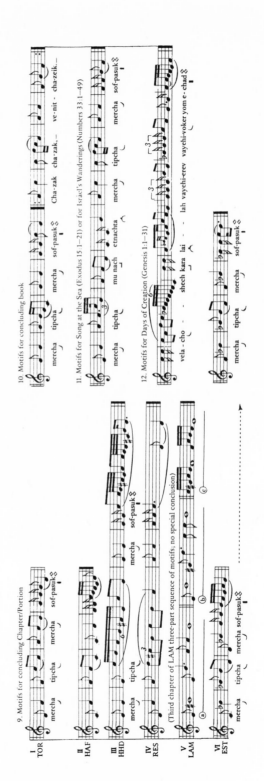

APPENDIX C

Appendix C shows 39 *Misinai* Tunes regularly used for chanting prayers, all transcribed at the same pitch level for comparative purposes. The left-hand column charts the Primary Occurrence of each *Misinai* Tune within the 18 Prayer-types listed in Example 3.11. For instance, Tunes ⟨1⟩ through ⟨4⟩ are *Barechu*-types (-a-), occurring primarily in the 'Call to Prayer' proper or shortly thereafter in Maariv. Tunes ⟨15⟩ through ⟨18⟩ are *Me'orah*-types (-g-), occurring primarily in Category II. Laudatory Poems (*Piyyutim*), inserted after the blessing, *Yotseir Or* ('Creator of Light'), in Shacharit, and so on.

The middle column gives 67 Recurrences of *Misinai* Tunes in sections of the liturgy other than their Prayer-type. Tune ⟨1⟩, for instance, a *Barechu*-type (-a-) recurs as a Category III. Penitential Lament (*Selichah*), 'Grouped Composed Verses'-type (-r-). Not all Recurrences fall under the 18 Prayer-types. For example, the first Recurrence of Tune ⟨3⟩ is from the *Pesukei Dezimra* ('Passages of Song') preliminary section of Shacharit; the second Recurrence of Tune ⟨5⟩ is from the Torah service, etc. The 67 Recurrences shown merely scratch the surface of possibilities, answering the question: Where? rather than: Which? They suggest—rather than show—places where *Misinai* Tunes traditionally recur.

The right-hand column cites 54 Parallels of the *Misinai* Tunes in Bible reading, Minnesong, and Catholic and Arabic sacred and secular usage. Most of these Parallels come from eight sources, the diaspora traditions of Bible reading, abbreviated at the upper left of each musical illustration as follows:

A Lith (American Lithuanian)

E Seph (Eastern Sephardic)

F Seph (French Sephardic)

5 (Five diaspora communities)

Ger (German)

Lith (Lithuanian)

16 (Sixteen diaspora communities)

W Seph (Western Sephardic)

Underneath each tradition appears a type of reading, also abbreviated (refer to the explanatory note preceding Appendix B). JUB indicates Jubilatory treatment of a passage. Thus for Tune $\boxed{1}$, the first Parallels citation, ^{Lith}RES indicates the Lithuanian tradition for chanting a passage from Ruth, Ecclesiastes, or the Song of Solomon during a Festival. The second Parallels citation for Tune $\boxed{21}$, $^{\text{W Seph}}$JUB/TOR, shows the Western Sephardic tradition for chanting a Torah passage in Jubilatory fashion.

Published sources for the *Misinai* Tunes, their Recurrences, and their Parallels, appear in abbreviated form at the upper right of each musical illustration. Information includes author, date of publication, and item or page number. A full bibliography of these sources, listed alphabetically by author, follows.

ALTER, Israel: New York, Cantors Assembly.
    1968   *The Sabbath Service.*
    1971   *The High Holy Day Service.*

BAER, Abraham: Gothenburg, the Author.
    1877   *Ba'al T'fillah.*

BINDER, Abraham Wolf: New York, Philosophical.
    1959   *Biblical Chant.*

BIRNBAUM, Abraham Ber: Czestochowa, the Author.
    1912   *Amanut Hachazanut.*

BLOCH, Ernest: Boston, Birchard.
    1934   *Avodath Hakodesh.*

COHEN, Francis Lyon: London, Funk & Wagnalls.
    1903   "Cantillation," *Jewish Encyclopedia.*

COHON, Baruch Joseph: Cincinnati, Publications for Judaism.
    1951   *The Jewish Song Book* (after Idelsohn).

DAVID, Samuel: Paris, Durlacher.
    1895   *Musique Religieuse.*

EPHROS, Gershon: New York, Bloch.
    1953   "Yom Kippur," *Cantorial Anthology, II.*

FRIEDMANN, Aron: Berlin, Israelitischen Gemeindebunde.
    1901   *Schir Lisch'laumau.*

GENNRICH, Friedrich: Cologne, Volk.
1951   "Troubadors, Trouvères, Minne-und Meistergesang,"
       Das Musikwerk.

GEROVITCH, Eliezer: Rostow-on-Don, the Author.
1890   *Shire T'filoh.*

GLANTZ, Leib: Tel Aviv, Israel Music Institute.
1968   *Hallel & Three Festivals.*

GOWSEIOW, Jacob: St. Louis, Halpern Foundation.
1966   *Neginot Yaakov, II.*

HAGEN, V.d.: Hanover, the Author.
1841   *Die Minnesaenger, IV*

HELLER Josef: Brno, Winiken.
1914   *Kol T'hillah,II.*

IDELSOHN, Abraham Zvi: Tel Aviv, Dvir.
1924   *Toledot Haneginah Ha'ivrit*

       New York, Holt.
1929   *Jewish Music*

       Leipzig, Hofmeister.
1932a "Synagogue Songs of the German Jews,"
       Thesaurus of Hebrew Oriental Melodies, VI.
1932b "Synagogue Song of the East European Jews,"
       Thesaurus of Hebrew Oriental Melodies, VIII.
1933   "Traditional Songs of the South German Jews,"
       Thesaurus of Hebrew Oriental Melodies, VII.

JAPHET, Israel Mayer: Frankfurt, Kaufmann.
1881   *Schirei Jeschurun.*

KAMIEN, Roger: New York, Norton.
1970   *The Norton Scores.*

KATCHKO, Adolph: New York, Hebrew Union College.
1952   *Thesaurus of Contorial Liturgy, I.*

KOHN, Maier: Munich, Synagogen-Chor-Comitei.
1839   *Vollstaendiger Jahrgang, II.*

KOUSSEVITSKY, Moshe: New York, Tara.
1977   *From the Repertoire of Cantor Moshe Koussevitsky.*

LEVINE, Joseph A.: (Baltimore Hebrew College) ,Ann Arbor,
       University Microfilms.
1981   *Emunat Abba I & II* (after Weisgal).

LEWANDOWSKY, Louis: Berlin, the Author.
1871   *Kol Rinnah Ut'fillah.*

LIBER USUALIS: New York, Desclée.
1956, edited by Benedictines of Solèsmes Abbey.

LOEWENSTAMM, Max G.: Leipzig, Kaufmann.
1882   *S'miroth L'El Chaj.*

NATHANSON, Moshe: New York, Hebrew Publishing.
1928   "Neginoth Hat'amim," *Pentateuch and Haftorahs,*
edited by Alexander Harkavy.

NAUMBOURG, Samuel: Paris, the Author.
1847   *Chants Liturgiques des Grandes Fêtes.*

NE'EMAN, Yehoshua Leib: Jerusalem, Israel Institute.
1968   *Nosach Lachazan.*

OGUTSCH, Fabian: Frankfurt, Kaufmann.
1930   *Der Frankfurter Kantor.*

ROSENBLATT, Yossele: New York, Metro.
1927   *Tefiloth Josef.*

ROSOWSKY, Solomon: New York, Jewish Theological Seminary.
1958   *Neume Motifs for the Yearly Cycle of Biblical Chant
According to the Lithuanian Tradition* , after manuscripts.

SCHAPOSCHNIK, Gershon: New York, Cantors Assembly (reprint).
c. 1960 *Hazzanic Recitatives.*

SCHNIPELISKY, Elias: New York, Metro.
1949   *Nishmas Eliyohu.*

SCHORR, Israel: New York, Bloch.
1928   *N'ginoth Baruch Schorr.*

SPECTOR, Johanna L.: New York, *Jewish Music Notes.*
Oct. 1950 "The Kol Nidre—at Least 1200 Years Old."

SULZER, Salomon: (Vienna, 1839-1865), the Author.
1905   *Schir Zion*, revised by Joseph Sulzer.

VINAVER, Chemjo: New York, Marks.
1955   *Anthology of Jewish Music.*

WAGNER, Peter: Freiburg, Veith.
1895   "Ursprung und Entwicklung der liturgischen Gesangformen," *Einführung in die Gregorianischen Melodien, I.*

WEINTRAUB, Hirsch: Koenigsburg, the Author.
1859   *Schire Beth Adonai, I & II.*

WEISGAL, Adolph J.: Baltimore, the Author.
1950   *Shirei Hayyim Ve-emunah.*

WEISSER, Joshua: New York, Metro.
1940   *Baal-T'filo, II.*

WERNER, Eric: University Park, Penn. State University.
1976   *A Voice Still Heard.*

WODAK, Meyer: Vienna, the Author.
1897   *Hamnazeach*

APPENDIX C

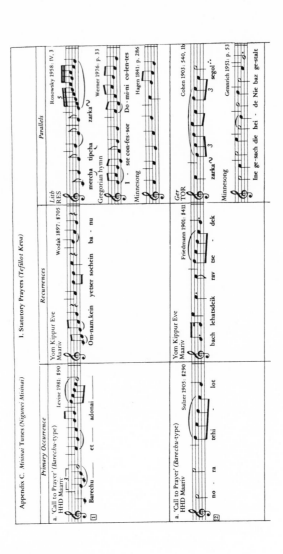

Appendix C. Misinai Tunes (Niggunei Misinai)

I. Statutory Prayers (Tefillot Keva)

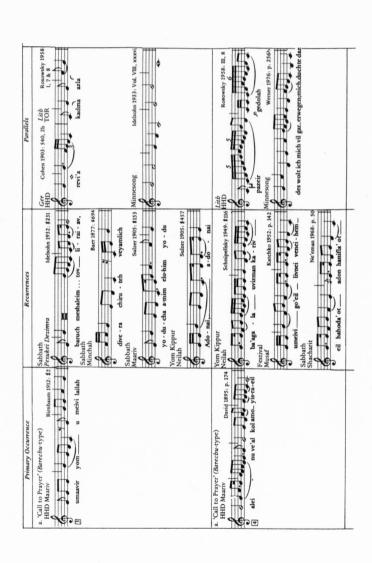

Appendix C • 219

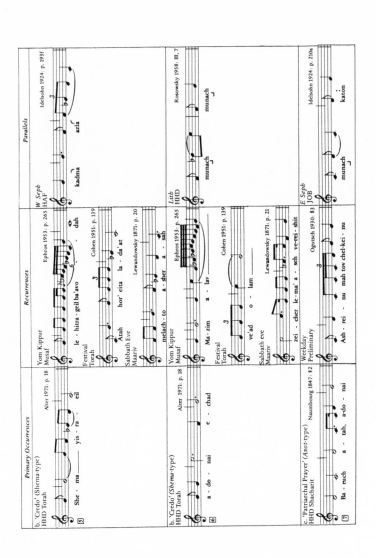

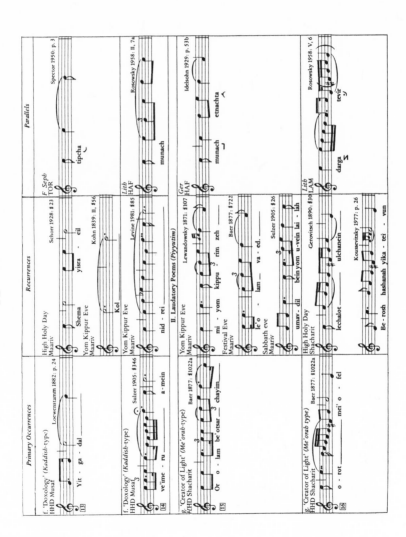

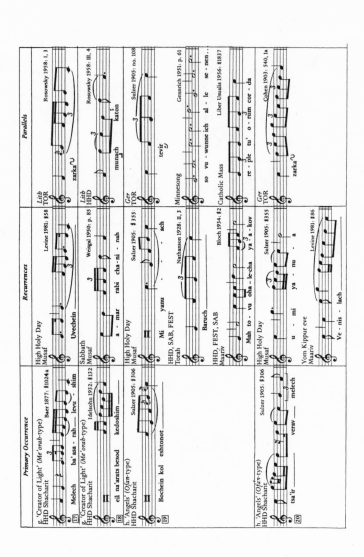

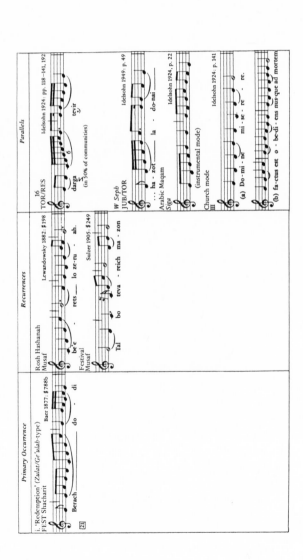

Primary Occurrence
Recurrences
Parallels
j. 'Divine Permission' (Reshut-type)
HHD Musaf
Weintraub 1859: p. 162
22
Ochi - lah la'eil achaleh fa - nav
Rosh Hashanah
Musaf
Idelsohn 1932: VI, p. 198
berak hashanun
Festival
Shacharit
Glantz 1968: p. 15
et hahal - leil.
Sabbath eve
Maariv
Alter 1968: p. 12
Eil chai vekayam
W Seph
HAF
Cohen 1903: 541, 3c
mahpach pashta
A. Lith
HAF
Binder 1959: 118b
kadma mahpach
k. 'Shield of Abraham' (Magein-type)
FEST Musaf
Baer 1877: #837
23
Be - da - to a - bi - ah chi - dot
High Holy Day
Musaf
Sulzer 1905: #354
Mi yich - yeh
Yom Kippur
Neilah
Levine 1981: #161
En - kat mesale - de - cha
Lith
LAM
Rosowsky 1958: V, 9a Chap. 3 only
A - ni hagever ra'ah oni . . .
Arabic Prayer Call
Idelsohn 1924: p. 26
la i - lah il - la al - lah
l. 'Resurrection' (Mechayeb-type)
FEST Musaf
Levine 1981: #437
24
Tal ya' a - sis tsuf ha - rim
High Holy Day
Musaf
Rosenblatt 1927: #21
Hi - ne - ni
Lith
HHD
Rosowsky 1958: III, 7a
munach
l. 'Resurrection' (Mechayeb-type)
FEST Musaf
Sulzer 1905: after #242
25
lir - si - so ke-su - fim
Month of Elul
Pre-dawn
Levine 1981: #3
hachi - no - ta ma'or vasha - mesh
Sabbath eve
Maariv
Koussevitsky 1977: p. 7
veyanu - chu vahyisra - eil
Ger
TOR
Cohen 1903: 543, 1a/544, 1a
munach geireish

Appendix C • 225

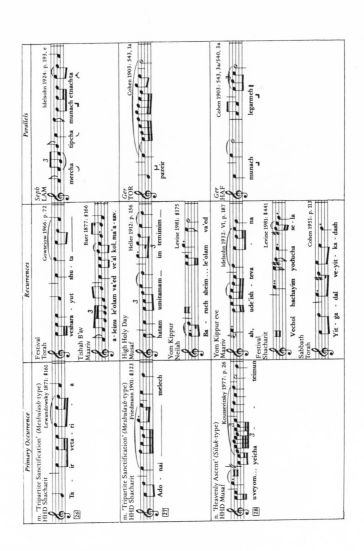

III. Penitential Laments (Selichot)

Primary Occurrence	Recurrences	Parallels

o. 'Individual Biblical Verse' (*Pasuk*-type)
Yom Kippur Eve
Gerovitsch 1890: #3

HHD and FEST
Musaf
Baer 1877: #862

Ger
TOR
Cohen 1903: 540, 1b

[29] mimisra - yim ve'ad   hei - nu.

Ah,   ah,

munach   revi'a

p. 'Grouped Biblical Verses' (*Sidrei Pesukim*-type)
Month of Elul: Pre-dawn
Weisgal 1950: p. 16

High Holy Day
Shacharit
Baer 1877: #1102a

Ger
TOR
Cohen 1903: 543, 1a

[30] a - do - nai   elo-hei - nu.

a - do - nai   yim 3 - loch

gedolah 3

HHD, FEST, SAB
Torah
Levine 1981: #349

Minnesong
Gennrich 1951: p. 58

ve - no' -   mari: A - mein.

Scan - den wol   vuor - sa - get

q. 'Individual Composed Verse' (*Selichab*-type)
Yom Kippur Eve
Sulzer 1905: #413a

Yom Kippur Eve
Maariv
Sulzer 1905: p. 495

Litb
HHD
Rosowsky 1958. III, 4, 3

[31] selach   la   nu

Shevi -   kin

mahpach pashta   segol

q. 'Individual Composed Verse' (*Selichab*-type)
Yom Kippur Eve
Wodak 1897: #702

High Holy Day
Maariv
Sulzer 1905: #295

Litb
JUB/TOR
Rosowsky 1958. I, 12

[32] mimisra - yim ve'ad   hei - nah

ve - higi - a   nu

vela - cho -   shech

r. 'Grouped Composed Verses' (*Sidrei/Selichbot*-type)
Yom Kippur Eve
Baer 1877: #1310e

Yom Kippur Eve
Maariv
Sulzer 1905: #401

Ger
TOR
Cohen 1903:542, 1a

[33] 'la a - vor   pesha

Ya -   a - lch

gadol —— (reversed) —— mahpach

Litb
TOR
Rosowsky 1958: I, 4c

Rosh Hashanah
Musaf
Baer 1877: #1247

be - sim - chat   o - lam

li:

r. 'Grouped Composed Verses' (*Sidrei/Selichbot*-type)
Yom Kippur Eve
Naumbourg 1847: #261d

Yom Kippur
Maariv
Levine 1981: #7

Litb
HAF
Rosowsky 1958. II, 8e

[34] ke - yom

she - losh   esreh

gedolah 3

Index

Synagogue Song in America

Cassette Album

Three one-hour audio cassettes in an attractive vinyl binder contain beautifully recorded performances of musical examples from the book. To order send $25.00 + $2.00 shipping to White Cliffs Media Company, P.O. Box 561-E, Crown Point, IN 46307